A History of Drug Use in Sport 1876–1976

This book offers a new history of drug use in sport. It argues that the idea of taking drugs to enhance performance has not always been the crisis or 'evil' we now think it is. Instead, the late nineteenth century was a time of some experimentation and innovation largely unhindered by talk of cheating or health risks. By the interwar period, experiments had been modernised in the new laboratories of exercise physiologists. Still there was very little sense that this was contrary to the ethics or spirit of sport. Sports, drugs and science were closely linked for over half a century.

The Second World War provided the impetus for both increased use of drugs and the emergence of an anti-doping response. By the end of the 1950s a new framework of ethics was being imposed on the drugs question that constructed doping in highly emotive terms as an 'evil'. Alongside this emerged the science and procedural bureaucracy of testing. The years up to 1976 laid the foundations for four decades of anti-doping. This book offers a detailed and critical understanding of who was involved, what they were trying to achieve, why they set about this task and the context in which they worked. By doing so, it reconsiders the classic dichotomy of 'good anti-doping' up against 'evil doping'.

Paul Dimeo is Lecturer in Sports Studies at the University of Stirling.

A History of Drug Use in Sport 1876–1976

Beyond Good and Evil

Paul Dimeo

Routledge
Taylor & Francis Group

LONDON AND NEW YORK

First published 2007
by Routledge
2 Park Square, Milton Park, Abingdon, Oxon, OX14 4RN

Simultaneously published in the USA and Canada
by Routledge
270 Madison Avenue, New York, NY 10016

Routledge is an imprint of the Taylor & Francis Group, an informa business

Typeset in Goudy by
GreenGate Publishing Services, Tonbridge, Kent
Printed and bound in Great Britain by
TJ International Ltd, Padstow, Cornwall

British Library Cataloguing in Publication Data
A catalogue record for this book is available from the British Library

Library of Congress Cataloging in Publication Data
Dimeo, Paul, 1971-
A history of drug use in sport 1876–1976: beyond good and evil/Paul Dimeo.
p. cm.
ISBN 978–0-415–35771–5 (hardcover) – ISBN 978–0-415–35772–2 (softcover)
1. Doping in sports–History. 2. Athletes–Drug use – History. I. Title.
RC1230.D5668 2007
362.29–dc22
2007001866

ISBN 978–0–415–35771–5 hbk
ISBN 978–0–415–35772–2 pbk
ISBN 978–0–203–00370–1 ebk

For Sally, Florence and Carla

Contents

Acknowledgements

This book was made possible by a period of research leave from the University of Stirling. I would like to thank colleagues who supported that leave by covering my teaching during that semester, in particular Judith Ramsay and Fiona Reid. Others in the Department have shown an interest in my research, passed on references and lent me books. Thanks also to Joyce Kay who read an early draft and suggested structural as well as (many) grammatical improvements.

I should also thank the following people for pointing out useful references: Rob Beamish, John Bale, Dave Terry, Peter Mewett, and Neal Garnham. Various sports history colleagues have helped me focus ideas and follow up new ones. I am also very grateful for the time taken by Derek Casey, Michele Verroken and Andrew Kicman to share with me their experiences and insights. In terms of getting access to source material, I found the on-line resource provided by the Amateur Athletic Foundation of Los Angeles (www.aafla.org) very useful. The archivists at the IOC Museum in Lausanne provided me with access to books and committee minutes. Members of staff at the University of Stirling's library were most helpful in finding inter-library loans. I am also grateful to the staff involved with the book at Routledge and GreenGate who provided an efficient and professional service.

Finally, on a more personal note, I'd like to thank my father who has always offered me his unconditional support.

Abbreviations

IOC	International Olympic Committee
CoE	Council of Europe
BANC	British Association of National Coaches
BASM	British Association of Sports Medicine
AMA	American Medical Association
ACSM	American College of Sports Medicine
FMSI	Federazione Medico-Sportiva Italiana
ANEP	Association Nationale de l'Éducation Physique
ICSS	International Congress for Sports Sciences
FIMS	Fédération Internationale de Médicine Sportive
NOC	National Olympic Committee
UCI	Union Cycliste Internationale
WADA	World Anti-Doping Agency

Prologue

The origins of this research can be traced to my career change in 2002 when I left University College Northampton and took up a position at the University of Stirling. I had been reading around in sports history, thinking of getting into the methodological debates then emerging on textuality, discourse and representation. The question of doping and anti-doping seemed ripe for a deconstructionist-type approach that unpicked the cultural and political values underpinning the ostensibly 'good' anti-doping ideology. In part, that sort of approach has informed this book. However, it was frustrating to read, in so many different places, passages of historical narrative that failed to meet even the most fundamental requirements of reasonably good historiography. They did not use primary sources, they unquestioningly repeated secondary sources that contained no evidence, they used invented stories from the past to prove points about the present, and they failed to ask any contextual questions. It seemed to me that the very least sports history as a discipline should have offered by now was a good narrative account of the rise of both doping and anti-doping based on solid, empirical information. The next stage would be to ask the obvious questions: where did drugs come from and why were they banned?

I hope that for both questions the book offers a whole raft of new information that denies easy answers. It would be tempting to say that doping came from professionalism or from sports medicine or athletes' obsessive desire to win. But such one-dimensional explanations avoid the complexities of the changing situations and shifting meanings surrounding drug use in sport. They also avoid a proper assessment of the links between scientific innovation and sports performance. The reader will find that scientists feature heavily in this book: this rebalances the tendency in sports history towards cultural and social analyses that forget science is also a cultural and social activity. In terms of anti-doping, the simple explanation is that there was an obvious problem that was corrupting the ideals of sport while at the same time risking the health of athletes. But what if both of these theories can be critically unpicked? The ideals of sport are, like science, a cultural and social product. There is no 'true' sense of sporting ideals, just a constantly shifting set of principles bought into and promoted by certain sections of society. The same goes for health, despite the apparently common sense of doping as a risky practice. Many sports inherently contain health risks, and many less risky sports still have unhealthy practices. The question then becomes: why the panicky, anxiety-ridden fuss over drugs?

By restricting the time frame, this book offers a detailed exploration of doping and anti-doping. In one sense, it would be easy to imagine that very little happens before 1976. Most of the major scandals did not come until the 1980s. Perhaps that is why historical information is so thin on the ground. Yet, as will be shown, there is a rich and complex history that needs to be explored. It is imperative that we learn about the processes and developments that set the agenda and the ideological map for later anti-doping. We need to know why anti-doping has become so bound up with a traditionalist view of sportsmanship, fair play and the altogether 'good' of sport. We need to know where doping came from and why certain people worked so hard to control it. This should help understand the predicaments of current debates and future directions. No less importantly, I hope it will read as good history.

1 Sport, drugs and society

Introduction

This history of doping in sport begins in 1876 with a highly distinguished Professor of Medicine taking his students on walks around Edinburgh and hiking with friends up a Scottish mountain to discover the properties of South American coca leaves, the constituent source of cocaine (not to be confused with the different and milder cocoa). The results were published in the esteemed *British Medical Journal* (Christison 1876) as interest grew in finding drugs that would relieve fatigue in workers, soldiers, the general population and athletes (Rabinbach 1992). It will end a hundred years later with a highly scientific set of tests for steroids introduced to the 1976 Montreal Olympics, an ethical system prohibiting drug use, and a secretive world of research, black market suppliers and self-experimenting athletes keen to find the next drug and to beat the testers.

This book sets out to explain what happened in the intervening century. To ask what turned the socially approved quest for stimulants into a tense stand-off between 'official' sanctions and 'unofficial' doping. This is a remarkable, fascinating history of the fantasy of performance set against the fantasy of morally pure sport. However, it is not simply a tragic tale of how sport was 'infected' by corrupt forces. It is not simply a moral tale of 'good' anti-doping up against 'evil' doping. In fact, that very picture of drugs and sport in history needs to be reconsidered.

Heroes and villains

Perhaps it is inevitable that most of the research and writing in this area is devoted to finding solutions to the 'problem' of doping. The unquestioned beliefs underpinning this approach are that sport should be about fair play, that all drugs are a form of cheating, and that athletes will be physically and morally damaged by drugs. This is the traditional, standard orthodoxy on anti-doping. It has led to a certain fashion for looking back through history to distinguish between heroes and villains. Much of the doping debate takes place in public forums as the popular media tends to try and work out who was 'guilty'. The on-going arguments about whether the American athletes Florence Griffith-Joyner and Carl Lewis used steroids illustrate this point (see Denham 1999, 2000, 2004). High profile accusations have been made about Linford Christie, Lance Armstrong and Marion Jones in the past couple of years. Going back to the 1970s and 1980s, we see that the GDR and USSR systems are consistently assumed to have been based on comprehensive doping (Ungerleider 2001). And the sudden rise of successful Chinese swimmers and runners in the 1990s was implicitly linked by some to illicit drug use. Such cases show how embedded the ethics of doping have become in global sports cultures and how many writers assume the simple good or bad model can and should be applied.

The sports philosopher Mike MacNamee (cited in BBC 2005a) has described the anti-doping movement as 'heroic' not least given the constant struggle to control new drugs and techniques. No one, as far as I am aware, has described a drug-using athlete[1] as 'heroic'. Instead this is a drama of straightforward characters, almost like a comic-book of 'good' crusaders up against dastardly 'evil' villains. This point is captured in one prominent visual example. When the Sports Council in Britain had a conference on doping in 1986, the front cover of the proceedings had the Biblical story of David and Goliath with the former looking up nervously at his enemy and saying, 'The only thing that niggles at the back of my mind is if God is on our side, why did he give them the anabolic steroids' (Sports Council 1986). Only two years later, the Ben Johnson episode at the 1988 Soeul Olympics showed that someone who was regarded as a great hero one day, praised for running the most incredible 100 metres and being the fastest man in history, could suddenly be vilified. At the time, the highly reputed British coach, Ron Pickering said, 'Good should never give way to evil, and this is evil that is being exposed' (cited in BBC 2005b).

While such examples lie outwith the timeframe of this book, they do offer a valuable insight into the self-belief of sports doctors and policy makers working on promoting anti-doping that they were doing 'good' work and that anyone who took drugs was 'evil'. The Sports Council cartoon image reflected and reinforced a highly influential linguistic change that occurred in the early 1960s and which has come to structure academic and public representations of the doping/anti-doping dichotomy ever since. Before the early 1960s there had been no great public scandal relating to drug use and there were no sustained campaigns against it. There was in fact a comparatively balanced discussion in some media about what value certain drugs might have for athletes. Many experts were unsure if drugs were capable of enhancing performance or if they had any significant health effects, either positive or negative. Moreover, official institutions had promoted research into stimulant drugs that might be used in sport ever since the first experiments on coca in the 1870s. Even by the 1940s and 1950s, universities and governments worked together to discover if amphetamines were useful in warfare, work and in sport. Ivan Waddington (2000) is correct to question the social construction of the idea that doping was an evil. Therefore, this heroes and villains caricature is based on a poor understanding of history.

A number of powerful social myths have been associated with this caricature. Western media and sports organisations have been quick to point out the doping-related excesses of communist countries, especially the GDR and USSR. This association of drugs with exploitative totalitarian regimes has a predecessor in claims that the Nazis developed amphetamines and steroids in the 1930s and 1940s, and that Hitler ensured German athletes had access to doping drugs for the 1936 Olympics in Berlin. They seem to fit with other accusations about inhumane experiments conducted in prisoner of war camps by the Nazis, as well as fitting with simplistic stereotypes of totalitarian regimes (Dimeo 2006).

Such myths are also pinned to the notion that athletes take drugs because of one of the following reasons: they are forced to; they are given them without being told; the promise of wealth and social status; they are loyal to their country. These constructions present doping as a consequence of nationalism, commerce and/or professionalism. Drugs were, in this paradigm, intimately bound up with other elements that have supposedly ruined sport's innate values. Doping was (and still is) seen as a pathology, a disease, and has been described as a 'scourge', a 'plague', a 'cancer' as well as 'evil'. The usual assumption had tended to be that drugs were introduced by 'evil' regimes bent on exploiting international sport to promote political ideology, who took a callous approach to the health of their citizens. Dr John Zeigler, renowned as the sports medic who developed steroids for American athletes in the mid 1950s, claimed that a 'Russian Doctor I befriended told me that in his country an individual is worth absolutely nothing' (1984: 2). This sort of ideology has informed much discussion of doping and indeed Zeigler wrote this for one of the most famous books on the subject by Bob Goldman *et al. Death in the Locker Room* (1984).

The historical details and case studies presented in this book will show that attitudes towards performance aids and willingness to experiment with new techniques and substances have been a feature of modern sport since the late nineteenth century. The fact that 'new' drugs such as amphetamines and steroids arrived in the mid twentieth century only helped develop an aspect of sport – the search for performance-enhancing aids – that had been evident in various countries for several decades. It is highly misleading to present some countries as 'innocent' and some as 'guilty'. Or indeed to assume that it was just the 'modern' pressures of international elite sport that led to doping that made athletes use whatever science and the pharmaceutical industry was making available to them.

In fact, it could be claimed that instead of doping increasing because of available substances, the demand for such drugs by athletes was part of the social history of this scientific knowledge. Science does not exist in a social vacuum as simply nature revealing herself through the insight and labours of researchers. As the historians of science, Peter Bowler and Iwan Morus write:

> science is a human activity, not an automated process that could be done equally well by a giant computer. Philosophical commitments, religious beliefs, political values, and professional interests have all helped to shape the way scientists have constructed and promoted their models of the world.
>
> (2005: 16)

The heroes and villains are harder to separate in the history of doping science. Amphetamines were used as much by Allied forces in the Second World War as by their Axis enemies. Steroids were being experimented with in the USA by the 1930s and 1940s. Usage of steroids was not seen as problematic by Dr John Zeigler, the American weightlifting coach who helped develop the steroid Dianabol with the pharmaceutical company CIBA in the mid 1950s. Around the same time, the legendary 'hero' Roger Bannister who would help lead anti-doping in Britain in the 1970s experimented with extra oxygen inhalation for his mile runs. And throughout the post-war period those professional cyclists who used amphetamines and other drugs for their arduous races remained favourites with the fans who empathised with their need for artificial enhancements.

Heroes sometimes need to be recast as villains and vice versa. There is a much greater ambivalence to this history than the dichotomy of good and evil allows. Even the ostensibly 'good' side needs to be carefully analysed. Anti-doping cannot simply be imagined as a 'crusade' of heroes fighting selflessly to protect sport and the watching public. Again, the roles and attitudes of scientists as with policy makers need to be set in context. Anti-doping had its flaws – ideological, political, scientific and pragmatic. Individuals were motivated by their subjective opinions as well as opportunities for career advancement. It was not always an especially coherent movement. But we can say that there was radical change that occurred with the rise in anti-doping in the early 1960s, as campaigners collected their efforts, constructed a language to support these efforts, and developed the scientific, bureaucratic and legalistic mechanisms. This is a process that has been ignored in the historiography of sport and of medicine.

A central feature of this book is to developing a better understanding of the shift from the (at least, partial) legitimacy of doping to the 'official' consensus by the late 1960s that all doping was wrong. It does not assume that all drug takers are evil and all anti-doping campaigners good. Instead, the argument will be developed that anti-doping was about social power and was based on very specific Eurocentric, pseudo-religious morality linked with a romantic idealism about the function of sport in society. This took aim at the extreme end of unethical behaviour while a small minority argued (to little avail) that the problems lay not with a deviant fringe element but with the very logic at the heart of sport itself.

History of doping and anti-doping: evidence and methods

While there has been a great deal of research and conceptual analysis of doping and anti-doping, there has been an absence of detailed historical analysis. The exception to this general rule is the work of John Hoberman who has produced a range of books and articles addressing the development of doping and the anti-doping movement (1992, 2005). Through rigorous research, asking the hard questions while retaining a detached scepticism and an idealistic view that sport should be better, Hoberman has advanced our knowledge of historical issues more significantly than any other contributor. Even so, there has been no attempt at a linear history – a narrative of events and people that would reflect a 'traditional' form of historiography that connects individuals to institutions and changing social conditions.

This is not necessarily straightforward. Evidence will always be partial, especially given the nature of the subject. People did not generally record or publicise their methods for outgunning the rest of the competitive field. Despite shifting perceptions of the legitimacy of doping, there was never a period of real transparency. The users of drugs have always been the rebels, the underground deviants, while those in charge of anti-doping have had moral authority and social power. They have recorded meetings, conferences, scientific analyses and been supported by media reportage. Given this, it is impossible to ignore the interconnection of power and representation: those with moral and legislative authority have used information processes to enhance their power and promote their message. So popular perception tends to reflect the ways in which anti-doping ideology and publicity has worked. This cannot be ignored in the construction of an empirical account. I do not wish to get drawn into a full debate here about historical methods, epistemology and the consequences of the 'cultural turn'. The approach here is pragmatic yet aware. In essence, a story has to be told, but myths and ideologies also have to be unpicked. I accept Doug Booth's (2005) point that language does not offer a window on to historical reality and historians cannot simply build up an unproblematic version of history based on textual sources. The documents used in this study are taken where appropriate as truthful representations, either in the truth of their production or of the straightforward facts they assert. That offers the chance to question the supposed truths that are being presented, while also recognising the influence texts can have even if they are factually incorrect.

The history of English cyclist Arthur Linton can serve as a brief illustration of this approach. One common myth is that he died of a drug overdose administered by his trainer. The leading academic in anti-doping policy, Barrie Houlihan, claims, 'The death of the cyclist Arthur Linton in 1886 may be the first recorded death of an athlete from an overdose of drugs' (1999: 34). To support this Houlihan cites a journal article called 'Drug Use and the Adolescent Athlete' in *Pediatric Annals* by P. G. Dyment (1984). Checking this article reveals the following statement, 'The first known fatality due to this form of cheating ['taking chemicals'] was an English cyclist who died after overdosing on trimethyl in 1886' (Dyment 1984: 602). It is a strange source for Houlihan to repeat. It does not mention Linton, does not offer any sources of evidence, and does not show that taking trimethyl was considered cheating in the 1880s.

Not only does Houlihan rely on this dubious secondary source, but he then shows uncertainty at the actual facts of the case. He cites – in the same footnote – Tom Donohoe and Neil Johnson's (1986) *Foul Play: Drug Abuse in Sports*, who 'suggest that Linton did not die during or close to competition but in fact died many years later from typhoid' (1999: 34). No author has produced documentary evidence either way, but Houlihan chooses the argument that suits his purpose which is to prove the historical continuity of doping. He even extends the point with some pure unsubstantiated speculation, 'Despite the publicity it generated, the death did little if anything to dissuade drug users. Reports of doping continued to appear throughout the remaining years of the century' (1999: 34).

So we know there is a process of invention and re-presentation going on here. Houlihan was not in a position to claim the death was 'recorded', that it generated publicity, that there were other drug users or that further reports of doping appeared anywhere. If one example of such misrepresentation is not enough, Ivan Waddington (2000) deals with Linton's death in exactly the same way: the claim of his 1886 demise from drugs in the text and oddly he also includes as an endnote Donohoe and Johnson's counterclaim. A slightly better informed source is Les Woodland's account of the history of cycling which tells a very different story. Linton, a Welsh (not English) amateur rider, was accused of using drugs during a race in 1896 though there was no physical evidence other than that he looked 'glassy eyed' and was 'trembling' during the race (2003: 19). The other circumstantial evidence was that Linton's trainer was 'Choppy' Wharburton who would provide his riders with a drink from a bottle with unknown contents. Woodland does not provide any primary source material but does have Linton in a race in 1896, ten years after Dyment, Houlihan and Waddington have him dead.

A search of media archives has provided a much more adequate sense of what happened to Linton. He was definitely alive until 1896, having won the amateur 12-hour Cuca Challenge Cup in 1893 and held the record in 1896 for the Paris–Bordeaux Race – 21 hours 17 mins for 591 km (*The Times*, 15 May 1897). He died in 1896 and according to his obituary, 'He had been for some days suffering from typhoid fever, and his physical strength had been much reduced by over-training' (*The Times*, 24 July 1896). This is the best evidence available and it suggests the sport itself more than drugs was responsible for his state of ill health. So we know more through late nineteenth century sources than the unquestioning repetition of secondary sources has provided. However, the full facts are still unknown and questions remain. It is possible that doctors could not tell the difference between drug-related symptoms and typhoid, or that just because he died of typhoid does not mean he was innocent of drug use. However, the point to make is clear: we cannot say that his death was due to drug use because there is no evidence either way. We definitely cannot say that it was 'recorded' as such, or that it was in 1886 because we do not have counter-evidence. Therefore we cannot interpret the fact of his death as proof of the continuity and health risks of doping in history. The 'deconstruction' of one mythical discourse has led, after a search for more plausible evidence, to the 'construction' of a better account, even if this is still only a partial and debatable explanation. We have not arrived at the truth or a 'window' on to the past, just an improvement on previous speculations and confusions.

Structure and themes

The book is divided into two parts: the first presents evidence-based examples, case studies and the history of doping science from the 1870s through to the

Second World War; the second deals with how doping became a 'crisis', both through the expansion of drug use and through the emergence and consolidation of anti-doping.

Part I

The beginnings of this story will be traced to the mid to late 1800s. Sport was beginning to be modernised through written rules, regulated spaces and times, organised competitions, international diffusion, creation of national teams, and international governing bodies (Guttmann 1978). At the same time, methods of industrial production were being re-examined in order to boost output and efficiency, the most notable example being Frederick Taylor's (1911) 'time and motion' studies. Middle-class reformists fretted over the health of the working classes and urban hygiene was less than ideal. As such, there was an influential movement towards reform, progress and modernity. Drugs and other substances with stimulant properties were viewed in a positive light, as having the potential to assist social reform by combating fatigue.

The circumstances for introducing drugs to athletes were therefore not just about winning events, but about making their bodies pinnacles of human achievement. The earliest doping products were based on drugs synthesised from South American and African plants, made into drinks and powders, and marketed as stimulants. Alcohol was also considered to be a stimulant and was regularly consumed by competitors (Collins and Vamplew 2002). Caffeine had been the fashion in high society across Europe and North America, and was praised for its stimulant properties (Hoberman 1992). By the late nineteenth century, cocaine was becoming more widely used including by such public celebrities as Sigmund Freud. Laudanum, coca, heroin, cocaine and opium were widely used.

There is not a great deal of evidence about drug use by athletes at this time. The 'potted history' approach of previous accounts based on unsubstantiated anecdotes and rumours serves only to show how little is known about this period. There are some prime examples though that can be discussed: the use of tonic drinks by Yale University and New York track and field teams, Thomas Hicks' encounter with strychnine and brandy in the 1904 Olympics marathon, Pietro Dorando's use of strychnine and atropine in the 1908 Olympic marathon and six-day cyclists hospitalised after drug use. These show that even from the early years of modern sport, athletes and their coaches turned to drugs to help their cause. These need to be understood in light of a specific set of meanings attached to drugs. This usage was not breaking any specific rules and was in the context of the spirit of nineteenth-century science.

Knowledge on how drugs worked and which ones would be useful for sport was in its infancy. The experimental work of French physiologist Philippe Tissié on the cyclist Stéphane shows that some scientists were more interested in using athletes as high performance guinea pigs to make discoveries about the drugs themselves (Hoberman 1992). At the other end of the spectrum, commercial companies tried to use athletes to advertise their tonic drinks. In between these extremes were athletes and their coaches whose sources of knowledge were as likely to be self-experiment and crude anecdotes as any proper empirical research. In the aftermath of Hicks' and Dorando's use of strychnine, clinical research showed that in small doses the drug could have a stimulant effect. In this case science lagged behind the real-life practice; athletes were beginning to search for the edge and waiting for science to confirm the properties of a drug was not an option.

The inherent optimism surrounding drugs in society in the mid nineteenth century to improve the human body and aid social progress was soon to be confronted with health and moral anxieties about drug use. Criticism came from temperance campaigners and those with other agendas about 'deviant groups'. Hand-wringing discourses on drug use among 'problem' social groups played on wider fears of crime and vice. Claims of addiction, sexual flagrancy, violence, murder and general social degeneracy, became integral to how drugs were understood in society. It suddenly became less fashionable to use drugs like cocaine and prominent individuals such as Freud changed their minds, criticised the drugs, and maintained a public silence on their earlier misadventures (Berridge 1999). In Britain the opium panic of the early twentieth century came to express social fears notably focusing on young working-class West End show girls and their various iniquities. Working-class mothers who gave opium to babies were another focus for reformists' zeal. These connected to white middle-class fears about other 'races': the 'oriental' opium dens and the black American jazz scene. In his book on this history, Marek Kohn suggests drugs 'permit the terrors of the social subconscious to be voiced' (1992: 2). So while sports doping had not yet prompted such moves it was inevitable that new ideas for enhancing performance would be framed by broader concerns about health, addiction and behaviour.

Moving into the interwar period, the premise on which drug use in sport was based was twofold: that they could be of benefit, but that health effects had to be carefully monitored. The idea that they were contrary to ideals of fair play and sportsmanship does not seem to have occurred to many involved. That did not lead to full openness about drug use though, and some examples show a lingering sense that the public and media might not see the drugs and performance issue from the athletes' and coaches' perspective. The International Olympic Committee (IOC) half-heartedly raised the issue at a meeting in 1938.

This period saw radical changes in sport, science and drug use. Sport was increasingly modernised in a number of important ways. Coaches introduced new training methods as scientists began to argue that the body could be adapted by discipline, skills training, and hard work (Beamish and Ritchie 2005). Exercise physiology groups developed, particularly in the USA and Germany, that sought to understand how the human body responded to various exogenous and endogenous changes. A number of sports had become increasingly popular, international, high profile and offered rewards of status and/or financial wealth to successful competitors. As an example, the Olympic Games moved out of the shadow of the World Fair movement to become an autonomous entity. In 1932, the host city of Los Angeles managed to make a profit from the Games and the copyrighting of the logo brought income to the IOC. In 1936, Adolf Hitler made a great propaganda show of hosting the Games in Berlin. Despite the successes of black American Jesse Owens, Germany topped the medal table and media representations aimed to reinforce their racial superiority. The Games were becoming commercial and political. Other sports were showing similar characteristics. The Tour de France had been established as the most prestigious of all major cycling events. The Football World Cup began in 1930. Sport was becoming modernised, global and financially successful – new technologies and preparation methods were commonplace as competitors tried to improve their levels of performance. The spectacle they created was increasingly attractive to the paying public, and athletic 'heroes' became national icons – a role which was exploited for commercial gain by endorsing products.

Meanwhile, athletes increasingly used 'artificial' enhancements, known at this time as 'ergogenic aids'. There is a lot more evidence from this period of such practices and attitudes. Some of the substances experimented with now seem bizarre: monkey gland extracts, sodium phosphates, bags of sugary sweets, ultraviolet light, and extra oxygen. However, some were more recognisable in today's lexicon of doping: cocaine, amphetamines, hormones, and caffeine. By the 1930s and 1940s a number of physiologists offered well-informed summaries of clinical research on the efficacy of a range of substances (Bøje 1939; Karpovich 1941). However, it was the research on amphetamines, especially in connection with wartime efforts, that brought to the attention of athletes one of the most powerful stimulants to enhance their performances. The symbiotic relationship of sports and war also linked to work; the central feature connecting these was fatigue and how it might be solved. The health aspects were assumed secondary to the demands of war. And since amphetamines were widely used in the general population for a range of medical problems and for relieving tiredness, little critical attention was given to their potential consequences. Physiologists tended to assume that any stimulant that was harmful should not be given to athletes but only offered mild warnings that amphetamines might cause excessive stress on the body as the natural sense of fatigue was by-passed. At this time, few expected amphetamines to cause any significant side effects.

So this period, from around 1930 to the end of the war, established a highly optimistic view of amphetamine use that would inform post-war athletes' use of stimulant drugs. There was also a strong suggestion that hormonal treatments would prove useful: an early sign of anabolic steroid use. As such, by the late 1940s there was a strong history of drug use and experimentation in sport. There had never been a 'golden age' of 'pure' sport. Instead, the determination and desire that comes with being an elite athlete led to the quest for pharmaceutical enhancements. Scientists were only too willing to help: it was in their interests to make new discoveries. The military demands for solutions to soldiers' fatigue also pushed forward research and knowledge. On the other hand, there were some concerns that overuse would lead to psychological and physiological problems. Scientists urged caution but the sports authorities were slow to react. The assumption was that this was not a major problem and that athletes had the good sense not to indulge in high risk drug taking. By the mid 1950s it was clear that neither of those assumptions was valid.

Part II

The post-war period up to 1976 was dominated by two main processes: the rise in drug usage, and the rise in anti-doping. The chapters in this part of the book take these in turn.

Amphetamines in sport developed out of the war and widespread public usage. Available evidence points towards two main places for this: American sport from high school up to professional; European sport, especially cycling. However, this usage was characterised by a profound sense of ambiguity as to whether or not it was 'wrong'. There were no laws against it and few doctors raised serious concerns about the health effects when used in medical dosages. The worst that could be said against amphetamines during the 1940s and 1950s was the following: they might be addictive, they might impair judgement, and they might introduce young people to dependency on drugs leading to more serious narcotics. However, the difference with athletes arguably was their propensity to overuse such drugs and to take them in situations of physical stress. The evidence of usage through the 1950s is extensive and shows how far athletes were prepared to go for sporting success. The idealism that sport should be a level playing field was not one that athletes took seriously. Usage continued through the 1960s and 1970s, with the most sensational episodes occurring in American professional sports and in European professional cycling. There were some cases of serious accidents and even fatalities being linked to amphetamine use in the 1950s and early 1960s (Council of Europe 1964). Yet, these did not prevent some users still openly discussing their habits – most notoriously the French five times winner of the Tour de France Jacques Anquetil argued that all professional cyclists took drugs and should be allowed to do so. The death of his colleague, Englishman Tommy Simpson in the 1967 Tour did little to prevent ongoing use by elite cyclists (Fotheringham 2003).

The emergence of anabolic steroids in sport is usually traced to American and Soviet weightlifting coaches in the mid 1950s. John Zeigler claimed that the Soviets were using testosterone and so worked with an American pharmaceutical company to develop and market the steroid Dianabol (Zeigler 1984; Voy 1991). This was in the wider context of developments in medical hormone treatment and commercial health products (Hoberman 2005). While steroids were initially used by bodybuilders and weightlifters, by the late 1960s they were much more popular among other athletes looking to build muscle and stamina during training. Steroids helped the user train for longer and can be stopped before an event, whereas amphetamines were used for the 'extra kick' just before or during the event. For instance, cyclists would keep theirs for the harder sections of a race or for the finishing stretch (Voet 2001). Steroids were taking over from amphetamines as the drug of choice by the late 1960s. Not only was there a test for amphetamines and not for steroids, but they were considered much more effective. The reaction from the scientific community was one of confusion (Taylor 1991). Studies on low doses did not show much of an effect or any obvious health problems, but athletes were actually using significantly higher and riskier doses. More than that, the health effects were long term, not the impaired judgement or dehydration found with amphetamine users. And steroids became more political – American coaches reasoned that if the Soviets had them 'our boys' should have them; some coaches and doctors actually saw it as their patriotic duty to supply the drugs (Goldman *et al.* 1984). Athletes were prepared to take the unknown risk for the sake of their career and the prestige it offered.

The most important change in the post-war period, one that changed the face of sport through intended and unintended processes, was the rise of anti-doping. It has been usually assumed that anti-doping was the work of 'heroes' responding to an obvious 'crisis' and organising means of protecting athletes. Indeed, the propaganda of anti-doping usually refers to the protection of young people from drugs, the protection of fair play in sport, and the protection of athletes' health (Waddington 2000). This is similar to the histories of other drugs, as Marek Kohn explains:

> Despite the political and social saliency of the issue today, public understanding of drugs rests on unsophisticated assumptions. Principal among them is the belief that drug laws reflect a sort of natural law; that the illegality of a number of chemicals is the necessary consequence of their inherent pharmacological properties.
>
> (1992: 1)

It is strange that the discourse of anti-doping has not been the focus of more critical dissection. Even from the earliest period of the 1950s and into the 1960s, anti-doping critics routinely called doping an 'evil'. The sense of morality and even of religious crusading underpins the history of anti-doping. Drugs users were portrayed as deceitful, immoral, and corrupt. And yet, drug use had been part of sport for decades, given explicit support from scientists and unhindered by sports' authorities interventions. The framework of sporting idealism – that it should be a level playing field – was imposed on the drugs issues by medical experts in the 1960s. It was an invention of the time. And yet, the professional networks, career status, wider social change and power relations involved have not been critically detailed.

The collection of data on doping first began in the mid 1950s. Italian scientists were concerned about accidents in cycling and set out to monitor and reduce drug usage. In America, surveys showed high levels of usage and studies of the effectiveness and health problems associated with amphetamine use were undertaken. The President of the IOC, Avery Brundage was concerned about the problem in 1960, and the death of Danish cyclist Knud Enemark Jensen during the Rome Games of that year prompted him to set up a doping commission and research team. By 1962, sports medics in Austria, France, Britain, Switzerland

and Italy were organising themselves and pressuring their national sports authorities to establish clear anti-doping rules. The Council of Europe (CoE) gathered these medics in 1963 at the first international conference on the subject and constructed the first international policy. The definition of doping used in that policy formed the basis for anti-doping throughout the world. A year later it was ratified by the IOC at their anti-doping meeting in Tokyo.

These were the formative years for anti-doping, when a small clique of medical experts campaigned against the problem but also defined it in scientific terms. Importantly this meant the solutions were to be scientific. No longer was the appeal to athletes' common sense enough, and no longer could governments be trusted to look after their athletes – suspicion was mostly directed at communist countries but Western governments have been equally as culpable through their hands-off approach. In the absence of adequate testing, scientists argued the case that the drugs simply did not work in the ways athletes believed them to, and hoped to see a decline. This was too optimistic: testing was eventually accepted as the real answer.

Perhaps the greatest untold story in this history is that it was British scientists who established testing procedures for both amphetamines and steroids. In 1965 it was Professor Arnold Beckett who led the first testing at major events: during the Tour of Britain cycle race. This was followed up by testing at the football World Cup in England in 1966. From there the test was implemented by the IOC at the 1968 Winter and Summer Games. Since the head of the doping commission set up by Brundage in 1962 was Arthur Porritt, who was also Chairman of the British Association of Sports Medicine (BASM), the feeding of British research to the IOC was easy and effective. Beckett, John Williams, and later Arthur Gold, were prominent figures in the CoE initiatives and in the IOC's Medical Commission that was established in 1967. The test for steroids was invented by Professor Raymond Brooks in 1974. This was first trialled at the Commonwealth Games that year, presented at a major international conference held by the BASM in 1975, and implemented by the IOC in the Games of 1976.

Anti-doping is therefore a construct of a specific time and place, not simply a response to a problem devoid of any historical context except the problem itself. The British scientists were motivated by a sense of duty and benevolence. Interestingly, the problem was usually defined as lying in other countries than Britain itself. At that stage, Britain was a fading power – both in the organisation of world sport, and in the general political economy of imperial power. The generation who promoted anti-doping has grown up in a social class-based world in which the ideals of the gentleman amateur sportsman still had a great deal of influence. It was a world in which British soldiers and scientists helped win a world war. It was also when the British sense of superiority was based on its Empire. And finally, this generation had a strong sense of Christian benevolence. In this context, anti-doping is an expression of a set of values that go far beyond the narrow question of drugs in sport. Or as Marek Kohn put it, 'the modern discourse about drugs is about far more than drugs, and these other themes are far more interesting than the drugs themselves' (1992: 1–2).

The scientists and policy advisors who promoted sport in mainland Europe were a more mixed group. However, they also had a strong cultural heritage of Christianity and indeed most were Catholic. Some of them came from countries that had Empires. There were significant differences to their British counterparts – mostly the closeness and obviousness of the problem to which they were responding: the health risks and deaths of cyclists. It is more difficult to assess the professional–amateur culture, as clearly cycling was a professional sport but when the IOC promoted anti-doping it tended to refer to amateurism as a closely fitted ideology. The other difference was the European tendency to construct bureaucratic organisations around anti-doping: from the CoE's meetings and policy to the IOC's Medical Commission. While the BASM did see anti-doping as central – it organised two major conferences in these early days of anti-doping (1967 and 1975) – there was no commission, sub-group or regular meetings. There were no positions as anti-doping officials in Britain: they joined in with other initiatives. Perhaps that explains why their role in the science of testing has been over-looked by academics and by IOC-oriented histories.

Critical perspectives on anti-doping and sport

Anti-doping changed the face of modern sport because it cast the shadow of suspicion over all athletes. Of course, the opposite might be argued, that testing was the best system of preventing wide-scale doping. But it was the very premise of anti-doping – that any drug taking was wrong – that set up an impossible situation. Even slight discrepancies, such as the ephedrine in a common cold treatment, could lead to lengthy bans. Drugs could not be used for short- or long-term recovery, pain management or building strength after an injury. This was an all or nothing strategy.

Moreover, the situation soon became unmanageable. First of all, drugs that had not yet been banned could be used without any positive results or punishments. Second, athletes and their doctors devised a whole range of 'detection avoidance' strategies. Third, with no out-of-competition testing, steroid use was going to happen as long as the athletes had proper advice for coming off them in time for the in-competition testing. In other words, by defining something as wrong, then being entirely incapable of stopping that happening, the suspicion is that sport since the 1950s had been largely fuelled by illegal drug use. It is really important that we have a better understanding of how anti-doping emerged, was consolidated and developed, in order to acknowledge why the mood of accusation and cynicism has prevailed since that time. At the same time, athletes could not compete at any level without being compelled to undertake a urine or blood test to 'prove' their 'innocence'. Sports authorities have had little to show for these tests, roughly 1 per cent of tests have provided a positive result: but the watching public know a much higher percentage than this have been guilty.

A related point is that testing created an unstoppable machine that in the twenty-first century is rapidly heading towards genetic manipulation as the cutting edge of performance enhancement (Miah 2004), and the past few years have seen designer steroids, EPO (erythropoietin, a naturally occurring hormone which can be injected to stimulate red blood cell production and so increase the flow of oxygen to the muscles), and human growth hormone being popularly used. These innovations may well have begun as far back as the 1870s, but by introducing bans and tests on available products, anti-doping created a market for new knowledge and new drugs. The test on amphetamines led to experimentation with steroids. The basic test for steroids developed by Raymond Brooks led to the use of testosterone in the late 1970s. And so in the 1980s Dan Duchaine's (1989) infamous and quite amazing *Underground Steroid Users' Handbook* was updated regularly with information on new drugs and new ways to beat the tests. Athletes have since revealed the intricacies of this culture of response, diversion, avoidance and innovation (Reiterer 2000).

Was there an alternative? Perhaps anti-doping could have used educational or sociological influences rather than be strictly scientific. Perhaps athletes could have been invited to the policy meetings on rule-making and on how the testing would be implemented. Perhaps a less naïve view would have predicted the outcomes noted above and not been as hopelessly optimistic as BASM Assistant Secretary and CoE anti-doping expert J. G. P. Williams was in 1967 when he predicted the amphetamine problem was solved, and the Chairman of the IOC Medical Commission Prince Alexandre de Merode was in 1976 when he thought testing would stop steroid use (Williams 1969; de Merode 1979). But what informed almost all anti-doping discourse was the idea that sport was essentially good and that doping was some form of corrupting, malign influence. Doping was seen as a cancer that might be cured through painful but necessary measures to restore the body to its usual glory. This was both a literal view of the sporting body and a metaphor for sport. Instead, as a few people at the time suggested, it was probably more realistic to argue that sport itself contained the seeds of its own doping-fuelled downfall. This is the central analytical theme of this history. The paradox was never resolved: whether sport was essentially good and doping was a temporary pathology that could be cured; or if doping was actually the direct, inevitable consequence of the will to win in sport, the scientific modernisation of sport and the rise of external rewards/pressures that drove people to cheat. While the more philosophical and health-oriented observers edged toward the latter, the pragmatic sports politicians and scientists promoted the former. As will be shown through the details of history, the ethics of sport were never fixed or final, they shifted with broad cultural and institutional changes, vested interests and specific agendas. This book sets out to describe and explain the emergence and growth of doping, and how and why the regulatory response came in the post-war period.

2 Doping and the rise of modern sport, 1876–1918

Introduction

It has been suggested that the early modern period of sport, roughly between the mid nineteenth century and the First World War, was a golden age unsullied by patriotism, commerce, intense personal rivalry, violence or drug abuse. When the French aristocrat and visionary Baron Pierre de Coubertin led the Olympic movement in the early 1890s he based it on romantic idealism. For him, sport could bring people from different cultures together and promote peace through healthy competition. This image of sport was inspired by his perception of sport in Ancient Greek society. He wrote in 1894 that the Greek heritage included 'training as a form of national defence ... the search for physical beauty and health through a delicate balance between mind and body ... that healthy drunkenness of the blood that has been called *joie de vivre*, and that exists nowhere else as intensely and as exquisitely as in exercising the body' (1894).

De Coubertin had come across the ways in which sport developed in the English public school system, and their mentality that sport taught discipline, co-operation and 'made men'. As such, he represented the section of the European middle and upper classes for whom sport was based on an amateur ethic, and sportsmanship was integral to being a gentleman. The most committed gentleman amateurs would shun any form of training, much less take drugs, as they considered such enhancements contrary to the spirit of sport. For them, it was an amusement, a distraction from the bigger things in life. It helped with fitness and sociability and – for the young especially – contained lessons for life. The conspicuous drive for achievement was 'bad form'.

As much as this group of sportsmen played their role in the development of sport, by the 1880s and 1890s a number of sports had professional players. Teams that represented cities or countries were, in sports such as football, supported by fanatics who invested results, victories and defeats with emotional value. This was the other face of sport: determined, socially symbolic, prestigious, and providing careers to successful competitors. There are numerous examples from a range of sports that detail the rise in serious sport from the end of the nineteenth century onwards. Just one might be the emergence of the fanatical and at times violent rivalry between supporters of the main Glasgow football clubs, Rangers and Celtic. Importantly, some sports such as cycling were professional and modernised from their origins.

It is tempting to suggest that drugs were a fringe element in sport, that it was the less noble participants who sullied the idealised image of sport with their skulduggery, or that drugs represented the cynical side of professional, career-oriented sport. However, it was hardly that simple. As will be shown, drugs that had the potential to safely assist physical and mental labours were actively sought-after by all classes in society, looking for ways to improve performance in work, war and in play. The examples of drug use in sport at this time were treated in diverse ways. Some contemporary accounts suggest openness to drug use and a desire to experiment. There were voices of criticism to be sure, and one can only speculate that if more cases of drug use were known there may have been more of a backlash. Certainly, the wider circumstances of drugs in society provided a more complex picture. The demands of social reform and industrial production meant drugs could be useful as a way to 'solve' fatigue, while traditionalists and temperance campaigners saw all manner of vices in drugs.

This is one of the most important chapters in the history of doping. It is the period in which drugs make their appearance in sport, and in which the science of doping is born. It set the tone for the twentieth century.

The science of doping

John Hoberman (1992) has argued that physiologists who experimented on the effects of drugs in sports performance were more interested in the drugs themselves than in how scientists could offer advice for improving performance. Indeed he goes so far as to conclude there was 'a sheer lack of interest in boosting athletic performance ... among the scientists of this period [late nineteenth century]' (1992: 128). Hoberman's illustrative example is the French scientist Philippe Tissié who used the elite cyclist Stéphane to test the properties of potential stimulants: tea, milk, mint water, lemonade, rum and champagne. But Tissié was not interested in helping Stéphane improve his cycling times. According to Hoberman, he 'considered athletic physiology only one approach among others to the study of the human organism' (1992: 127). Quite how representative Tissié is of European scientists is open to question. He almost became a fully fledged sports physiologist as the Olympic movement took off, but he distanced himself from what he saw as unhealthy practices of elite sport and thus from de Coubertin and the IOC. His interest in stimulants was tempered by scepticism about their benefits, their impact on health and the very nature of competitive sport. So, despite being 'the most important ... sports physician of the *fin de siècle*' (Hoberman 1992: 81) he represented only one strand of thinking and that was not shared by all scientists in Europe and North America who did envisage a closer relationship of sport and medicine.

Another scientist discussed by Hoberman is Gustave Le Bon, the French psychologist who showed an interest in kola nuts in the early 1890s. Having heard about the use of these nuts in Africa, Le Bon tried kola himself before conducting an experiment on the cyclist Charles Henry after which he concluded that kola was a 'powerful resource' (Hoberman 1992: 125). Keen to press the point, Hoberman argues that even by the later end of the 1890s 'there is no mention of giving kola to competitive athletes' (Hoberman 1992: 125).

However, this analysis has several flaws. Hoberman seems to miss the point that knowledge development was vital to doping, even if the application of the drugs was not the specific purpose. What scientists were aiming at provided assistance – inadvertently perhaps – to athletes seeking performance enhancement. These experiments gave scientific legitimacy to the idea of stimulants and the cyclists involved had an opportunity to test out specific substances. Other evidence shows that kola-based drinks were used by athletes, as will be described in the next section. Moreover, as Hoberman himself reveals, Le Bon's experiments were read by recreational athletes who tried out kola nuts themselves, so the impact (intended or otherwise) was to encourage usage.

More broadly, Hoberman failed to realise that other scientists were involved in this experimental research thus undermining his generalised conclusions based on two examples. During the period from the late 1850s to the 1880s European and American scientists conducted a series of experiments on potential stimulants. One substance of interest was the coca leaf from South America, the naturally occurring plant from which cocaine would be derived in the 1860s.

Anthropologists had described how indigenous people used coca to relieve fatigue and these findings were published in prominent European books and journals. The Italian scientist Dr Mantegazza made one of the first experimental studies in 1859 in which he explained that the leaf provided a 'strong tendency to muscular action, great vigour of mind, succeeded by a state of pleasing [and] imaginative calm' (cited in Christison 1876: 528). The leaf was becoming well known in scientific circles and had been mentioned by writers interested in stimulants and other drugs (Anstie 1864). It was one of the substances tested out on walkers by the Edinburgh doctor Alexander Bennett in the early 1870s. He showed it was a stimulant, as he also found were tea, coffee, theobromine and cocaine (1873, 1874; see Berridge 1999). The value of coca for pedestrianism was described by Weston who reported his findings in *The Lancet* and the *British Medical Journal* in 1876 (Berridge 1999: 217).

However, one of the most detailed and interesting studies was conducted by Sir Robert Christison. He was then one of Britain's most prestigious scientists: Professor of Medicine at the University of Edinburgh, Ordinary Physician to the Queen in Scotland, and President of the British Medical Association. He set out to discover the 'restorative and preservative virtues of the Peruvian cuca or coca-leaf against bodily fatigue from severe exercise' (1876: 527).

The first experiment in 1870 was conducted on two of his students who, out of the habit of exercise, tired themselves out by walking 16 miles. On their return, the doctor supplied them with 'two drachms of cuca' made with 'the addition of five grains of carbonate of soda' (1876: 529) to imitate the small quantity of lime or plant ashes used by local people in Peru to help chew the leaves [a drachm was 3–4 grams]. Christison reported that the students were rewarded with a stimulating effect: hunger and fatigue vanished and they comfortably walked for another hour. After this their hunger returned but they ate dinner, slept all night, and woke 'quite refreshed and active' (1876: 529).

Five years later, another batch of coca arrived, this time supplied by Alexander Bennett who obtained it in Paris, though of inferior quality to the earlier amounts. Ten students were asked to perform similar walking exercises to those in 1870 but of a longer distance, between 20 and 30 miles. Of these ten, two found that the coca had no effect, four had only moderate relief from fatigue, while the remaining four enjoyed their experience of coca, having completely recovered from fatigue. None had any 'disagreeable effects' except a 'brief nausea', which Christison attributed to the 'form of infusion' (1876: 529) rather than to the coca itself. Having observed no harm among his students, the time had come for some self-experimentation. In the beginning of May 1875, at the age of 78, Professor Christison walked a course of 15 miles, with no 'chemical' assistance, to gauge his levels of fitness. Four days later he walked the same distance, following the same diet as well, but during the final 45 minutes chewed 80 grains of coca. The result was that 'all sense of weariness had entirely fled, and that I could proceed not only with ease, but even with elasticity' (1876:530). After a comfortable six-mile walk he returned home, ate for the first time in nine hours, slept well and awoke with no sense of fatigue. He showed no signs of ill effect. Rather, one benefit was that a long-running problem with tenderness of the eyes had been 'very much mitigated during all the evening' (1876: 530).

Christison had some coca left which he took with him on holiday to the Scottish Trossachs in the autumn of 1875. With several companions he hiked up Ben Vorlich, a mountain of 3,224 feet beside Loch Earn. By the time they reached the summit, he was 'so fatigued that it required considerable determination to persevere during the last 300 feet' (1876: 530). Resting at this stage, his companions ate lunch while he instead chewed on two-thirds of one drachm, or 60 grains, of coca leaves. 'I at once felt that all fatigue was gone, and I went down the long descent with an ease like that which I used to enjoy in my mountainous rambles in my youth.' Returning to the foot of the mountain, he felt 'neither weary, nor hungry, nor thirsty, and felt as if I could easily walk home four miles' (1876: 530). Eight days later he repeated the experiment but with a larger dose of 90 grains. The effect was much the same, if slightly enhanced, though the four glasses of wine over dinner did not mix well with the coca causing a restless and feverish night. In fact, Christison's experiences mirrored Mantegazza's self-experiments in 1859 in which he showed that one or two drachms leads to 'an experience of warmth – I should say fibrilliform – spreading all over the body' (1859/1975: 38). And that two or four drachms produces 'the feeling of being isolated from the external world. One also feels deeply joyful and intensely alive ... the fullness of life is suffocating ... I feel extraordinarily agile when I take four drachms' (1859/1975: 39).

The conclusion of Christison's trials suggested that coca was useful for combating fatigue during exercise. Christison wrote that coca 'removes fatigue and prevents it ... no injury whatever is sustained at the time or subsequently ... it has no effect on the mental faculties except liberating them from the dullness and drowsiness which follow great bodily fatigue' (1876: 530).

The discussion of coca for athletes, and for physical stimulation in general, was fast becoming a hot topic in popular science. By the latter decades of the nineteenth century, coca was 'a novelty in European medicine' (Berridge 1999: 215). Commercial companies rushed to exploit it for the mass market, the most famous being Coca-Cola. By 1894 there were at least seven firms producing coca wine. The first of these was produced in 1863 by a Corsican pharmacist, Angelo Mariani, who patented a preparation of coca extract and Bordeaux wine. Vin Mariani was sold across Europe and the United States, 'promoted by a campaign keyed to youth, health, and celebrity endorsement' (Courtwright 2001: 47). The historian of drugs in the nineteenth and twentieth centuries, Virginia Berridge has described the fashion for such drinks as 'euphoria' (1999: 221). The most famous celebrity endorsement of coca and cocaine was that by Sigmund Freud who wrote a paper celebrating the drug's effects in 1884. Based on his knowledge of coca's use by labourers in South America, his own experiments and what he knew of other people's usage, Freud 'professed optimism about its potential to counteract nervous debility, indigestion, cachexia (wasting), morphine addiction, alcoholism, high-altitude asthma, and impotence' (Courtwright 2001: 48).

From 1885 the 'patent-medicine manufacturer' John Pemberton from Atlanta developed Coca-Cola to include 'at least two of the most effective stimulants then known to science: cocaine and caffeine' (Andrews and Solomon 1975: 10). In what now seems like an ill-considered move, Pemberton sold the trademark and formula to what is now the Coca-Cola Corporation. However, coca and its close chemical relation cocaine, were openly sold for a range of uses:

> Anybody could saunter into a drugstore and buy cocaine in a variety of forms. Indeed, it appeared in so many guises that the druggist might well have asked the customer whether it was wanted to be sniffed as a powder, nibbled as a bonbon, sucked as a lozenge, smoked as a coca-leaf cigarette, rubbed on the skin as an ointment, used as a painkilling gargle, inserted into bodily cavities as a suppository, or drunk as a thirst-quenching beverage such as Coca-Cola.
>
> (Andrews and Solomon 1975: 5)

The kola nut was also in vogue as shown by Gustave Le Bon's experiments. It was given scientific credibility through a range of studies. In the early 1890s, the President of the Homeopathic Pharmaceutic Association, J. C. Pottage, addressed the Annual Meeting and published his papers on the subject of kola, a substance found in West Africa and the West Indies which was viewed as similar to coca. Pottage described the Africans' view of it as a 'proved and permanent sustainer and restorer of human health and strength' (1891: 5). It was used by labourers to offset fatigue and maintain strength due to its high content of caffeine, 'the nuts contain more caffeine than coffee berries' (1891: 14). Kola was the basis of popular drinks such as Vino-Kolafra which was produced by the Brunswick Pharmaceutical Company and by Johnson & Johnson.

Pottage also saw commercial potential, claiming that the demand for kola 'will grow more and more as its valuable properties are better known'. He went on, 'I commend to those of our fellow-countrymen in our colonies and dependencies who desire to open up new sources of traffic, the consideration of how they may meet the increased demand for this product of tropical climates' (1891: 13). In his book on the subject, the first page was an advertisement of 'West African Kola Preparations', including 'Kola Elixir', for 'toning and strengthening the system'. Six years later, a meeting of the Royal Botanic Society confirmed that kola nuts were useful for stimulation and sustenance. A number of kola nut plants were propagated at Kew Gardens in the 1880s and distributed in turn throughout the British colonies. However, one of the purposes of this confirmation process was to validate the claims made by 'the Proprietors of Dr Tibbles' Vi-Cocoa' that it 'builds up strength and vigour by imparting nourishment' (*The Times*, 10 December 1897). This drink used kola and was marketed as 'cheap', 'palatable' and available to 'all classes from the highest to the lowest'. It acted to 'restore bodily vigour in whatever way jadedness or fatigue is brought about, and at the same time raise drooping spirits, and thus promotes the happiness of the people generally' (*Morning Post*, 29 November 1897).

In an article in the *Journal of the American Medical Association* in 1899, Dr Charles Yarborough praised kola as 'one of the most valuable drugs of our newer materia medica'. He argued it could be used for a range of therapeutic purposes, including pertussis, asthma, as a diuretic, and for melancholy. It was considered much better than alcohol and coca as it was not habit-forming, and it did not leave a depressive side effect after the initial stimulating effect. Overall, Yarborough saw kola as something of a wonder drug:

> The sustaining, strength-conserving power of kola, its characteristic action, makes it then of great importance as a therapeutic agent. It renders it peculiarly applicable to all those conditions where fatigue and exhaustion are imminent. Many physicians take advantage of this property of the drug to sustain themselves through extra and long-continued work, and especially if their duties call for loss of sleep.
>
> (1899: 1148–49)

Another drug that emerged in sport that was supported by scientific investigation was strychnine. During the nineteenth century strychnine was popularly held to be a stimulant in low doses and a poison in larger amounts. By the turn of the century, experimental research aimed to discover its properties. European scientists Rossi and Fere had found positive effects on fatigue and physical exercise. Fere found that 1 milligramme injected subcutaneously increased strength performance (cited in Rivers 1908). In 1908 a series of further tests were carried out by British scientist P. V. C. Jones, who gave subjects orally administered amounts of 4.2 milligrammes and conducted a muscular strength experiment. The increase in performance was initially substantial but over a longer period it actually diminished. These results were reported in the *Journal of Physiology*:

> The immediate effect is to produce an increase in the capacity for muscular work. With the smaller dose the increase is gradually produced with its maximum about three hours after its ingestion. With the 4.2 mgm. dose the maximum is obtained in about half an hour. In either case a fall follows and the capacity becomes subnormal – a condition which continued until the end of the experiment, a period of considerably over five hours.
>
> (Jones 1908: 445)

A summary of Rossi, Fere and Jones' work into strychnine was presented by W. H. R. Rivers, M.D. and Fellow of St John's College, Cambridge as part of a series of lectures delivered to the Royal College of Physicians in 1906 entitled *The Influence of Alcohol and Other Drugs on Fatigue* (Rivers 1908). It was concluded that strychnine produced a 'decided increase, followed by a reaction' (1908: 112). The medical historian John Haller has shown that strychnine had a wide range of uses and that by the end of the century had become 'one of the most powerful [drugs] in the physician's medical handbag' (1973: 236). Many of the applications were based on the idea that it 'provided general stimulation to the entire nervous system and markedly increased muscular tone' (1973: 235). As will be discussed below, athletes who used strychnine had this sort of outcome in mind. They did risk an adverse physical response though it is impossible to separate this from the normal fatigue that comes from excessive physical strain as will be caused by taking part in competitive events such as a marathon.

Rivers also investigated the effect of other drugs. He found that caffeine improved performance in an experiment of repetitive weight lifting by 20–30 per cent, though he warned that 'when taken in excess caffeine may act as an accelerator of fatigue' (1908: 38). Coca and cocaine were also discussed in positive terms. Rivers thought that cocaine had the greatest reputation of all the drugs that were alleged to reduce fatigue, and referred to previous studies showing its stimulating effect. Finally, he contested the claim that alcohol could boost physical performance. His first experiment showed an 'entirely negative result' while the second showed 'an immediate increase followed by a reaction shown in a fall below the normal' (1908: 70–1). He concluded that 'alcohol is prejudicial to the capacity for work and in no way helps to diminish the effects of fatigue' (1908: 88). Such prominent public dissemination of knowledge about stimulant drugs shows the link between science and social objectives in the quest for substances that could safely boost physical and mental capacity.

Drug use in sport

It would be wrong to claim that drugs were widely used in sport. There is not enough evidence to support this. However, the few examples available do show that one current of opinion at this time was to be optimistic and explicit about the potential for drugs to enhance performance. Of course, it can be disputed as to whether tonic drinks based on naturally occurring nuts and leafs are really forms of drugs. It is perhaps more realistic to consider them as naturally derived stimulants. Even so, the fact they were used means the attitude of the coaches and athletes involved was to use whatever aids they could find that might help. Moreover, some substances used such as strychnine must be considered to be a drug.

The tonic drink Vino-Kolafra was advertised in 1896 in an American sports magazine called *Outing* and in an accompanying article presented as a 'stimulant which serves its purposes without any ill effects, and the taking of which does not become a fixed and pernicious habit'. It had apparently been used with success by soldiers, the fatigued, the sick and 'the athletes of our leading colleges' for 'its marvellous sustaining power and its property of stimulating without the unpleasant reaction or depression that follows the use of other stimulants'. Among the benefits of kola were 'it is a mental exhilarant, overcoming despondency and brightening the intellect without resultant languor. It imparts tone to the muscular apparatus and secreting organs' (*Outing* 1896: 214).

The advertising claims included that it 'Stimulates Without Reaction' and that it 'Helped Win the Yale-Cambridge Games' as well as 'the games of the New York-London Athletic Clubs, and many other athletic contests during the past season'. On this latter point some further comment was made in *Outing*:

> the English athletes who were here at the international games last August marvelled at the condition of the American contestants. Their training appeared to be perfect, and the result was a long line of world record-breaking victories. The trainers who had the Americans in charge do not hesitate to say that the use of Vino-Kolafra by their young men was what made a large part of the wonderful difference in condition between them and their English cousins.
>
> (*Outing* 1896: 214)

There is no doubt that kola was being promoted here as both legitimate and as giving its users that 'extra edge' which would so trouble later campaigners against doping. At the same time, there was no attempt to disguise this drink as anything other than a drug. M. C. Murphy was trainer for Yale University and for the New York Athletic Club; his view was, 'I used Vino-Kolafra freely myself before giving it to my men. It acts on the nervous system, and in this way braces up the muscles … It certainly is a remarkable drug' (*Outing* 1896: 215). Other sources, including athletic coaches, military authorities and doctors testified to its value in combating fatigue and improving overall health. The basis for knowledge was the experimental work conducted in various countries by scientists interested in the 'medicinal value' of kola. Overall, this was a triumph for the manufacturers who were to be congratulated for:

Supplying to the world such an admirable tonic – one which strengthens the whole frame, a tonic which banishes weakness, whether physical, mental or moral, a tonic which will prove a priceless boon to all of the human family who struggle under adverse conditions with the heavy tasks of life.

(*Outing* 1896: 215)

Vino-Kolafra does not appear to have had an especially long history. Athletes widened their scope of interest regarding stimulants, and other, stronger, drugs were used. In December 1900 cyclists in an American six-day race ran into trouble when the drugs they used caused serious side effects (though what drug was used is not known). Only three of the seven pairs completed the race and three cyclists ended up in hospital where, according to the *New York Times*, 'a close inspection of the men was not an edifying spectacle'. Each rider had been 'liberally dosed with stimulating drugs', and they looked awful: 'their faces were lifeless, the muscles drawn and pinched, and eyes badly bloodshot' (*New York Times*, 16 December 1900).

The 1904 Thomas Hicks case is oft-repeated in doping histories: the American (though born in Birmingham, England) Olympic marathon winner who used brandy and strychnine. What has not been made clear so far are the details of this event nor how it was understood at the time. The race was overshadowed by the efforts of Fred Lorz, another American, to cheat in the race: he was driven part of the way in a car only to run the final five miles, arrive in the stadium as the apparent winner and take all the accolades from the unsuspecting crowds (Lucas 1905). The race was run over 24 miles and 1500 yards, Hicks was struggling even after 14 miles and his desperate request for a drink of water was refused by his coach. Three miles later he was given 'one-sixtieth grain of sulphate of strychnine, by the mouth, besides the white of one egg' by Charles Lucas who was a medical doctor travelling in a car with Hicks' coach Hugh C. McGrath and two companions – A. E. Johnson and George Hench (Lucas 1905: 52). Brandy was considered another option for stimulation though was not given at this stage. Hicks asked to lie down four miles from the end and his coach, Hugh C. McGrath of Charlesbank Gymnasium, Boston, refused to let him succumb in such a way for fear that he would not get up again. Lorz passed him at 19 miles even though Hicks seemed to have built a lead of one and a half miles. However, news of Lorz's deceit encouraged Hicks to keep running albeit slowly and looking on the verge of collapse. At 21 miles his 'ashen pale' state led to Lucas giving him 'another tablet of one-sixtieth grain strychnine' with two more eggs and a sip of brandy (Lucas 1905: 53). He stopped for a quick 'bathing with warm water' before struggling on despite looking dull, lustreless, heavy limbed, stiff and frequently expressing his hunger for food. With a mile and a half still to run he stopped again for brandy and to be bathed in warm water. He completed the race and was taken for a medical examination, which apparently found him to have no health problems except exhaustion. Certainly there is no evidence that the medics on scene took issue with the use of strychnine and brandy during the race (Lucas 1905). In fact, Charles Lucas argued that the reason Hicks won was that his opponents 'lacked proper care on the road' (1905: 55) and that after his strength had gone Hicks was 'kept in mechanical action by the use of drugs' (1905: 46). It is fascinating given the later discourses of drugs and cheating that Lorz is represented as defaming himself, his club and his country while Hicks is described as bringing 'the greatest honour ever brought to American shores by an American athlete' (Lucas 1905: 46). Drugs were not seen to be in any way problematic, indeed they hold the key to a closer relationship of sport and medicine, as according to Lucas, 'The marathon race, from a medical standpoint, demonstrated that drugs are of much benefit to athletes along the road' (1905: 52).

Critical voices

The question remains to what extent did drug use in sport trouble contemporary writers and participants. An early example of an emerging anti-doping ideology came in 1895 in an article in the medical section of the *New York Times*. This came in response to rumours of 'bicyclists who use various coca and kola compounds in order to help them with their work' and 'that preparations of cocaine are consumed to some extent'. These claims were treated with serious disapproval:

> We feel sure that all true athletes would disdain any such injurious and adventitious aids, but there is a vast number of persons who take such things thoughtlessly and injury is done thereby. The announcements which are made in advertisements of various stimulants, in which it is claimed that they save the strength and promote the endurance of bicyclers and athletes generally are very much to be deprecated. There are no drugs which will help one to win a game that could not be won without them, and the general effect of drug taking, and especially of the use of drugs belonging to the caffeine and cocaine class, is distinctly bad. We believe that the medical profession ought seriously to warn those with whom they come in contact professionally against the use of such things.
>
> (*New York Times*, 1 December 1895)

It was around the mid 1890s that one of the most public debates on doping took place. The cycling fraternity in England voiced criticism of the psychological trick devised by trainer 'Choppy' Warburton in which he gave his riders a drink of unknown properties in such a cloak-and-dagger manner as to suggest it contained something 'special'. Crowds of spectators accused his protégé James Michael of taking 'dope' during an 1896 race when he was seen taking a mouthful from Warburton's secret bottle. This was seen as part of a wider strategy employed by the trainer. The *Sporting Life* reported that another of Warburton's charges, Arthur Linton, had been repeatedly given strychnine, trimethyl and heroin (Woodland 2003). Whether or not the mysterious liquid contained drugs, it is clear that many of the watching fans and journalists took a critical view of this practice, even though no rules had yet been constructed to outlaw it. However, it seems just as possible that Warburton was employing the placebo effect. While some of the cyclists under his charge met early deaths, none have been shown to be caused by illicit drugs. Nonetheless, the trainer was banned from cycling tracks by the National Cyclists' Union. And we can see that doping was considered a serious breach of the 'spirit of sport' by at least some spectators during this period. Quite whether there is enough evidence to prove the case is doubtful. However, this obstacle has not prevented many writers from assuming Linton's death was caused by a drug overdose (see Chapter 1) or from claims such as Woodland's that Warburton 'had a reputation for using the drugs of the time to increase the tension of tired muscles (strychnine) and deaden the nerves (heroin)' (Woodland 2003: 19).

The most commonly cited example is that of Thomas Hicks, but the impression usually conveyed is that he suffered severe health effects and almost died as a result of the strychnine. For instance, Houlihan argues that he 'collapsed following the use of a strychnine-brandy cocktail' (1999: 34). Similarly, Terry Todd refuses to accept that Lucas' role and interpretation of the events might have been legitimate in historical context:

> The most famous case of drug enhancement occurred at the 1904 Olympic Games in St. Louis. The case is well known because at the conclusion of the marathon, the winner, America's Thomas Hicks, collapsed. During the investigation, Hicks's handlers, who had been allowed to accompany him throughout the course of the race in a motorcar, admitted they had given him repeated doses of strychnine and brandy to keep him on his feet. Even so Hicks's medal was not taken away, and his joy at winning was expressed to reporters in a telling way when he finally revived: "I would rather have won this race than be president of the United States".
>
> (Todd 1992: 323)

Todd's interpretation assumes that drug use ought to be seen as cheating, that some sort of investigation took place with that assumption in mind, and that Hicks could and should have been disqualified. However, since there were no rules against taking such drugs and the runner's 'handlers' were so honest about what happened, doping of this sort was probably not seen as a crime. Moreover, the testimony given by Charles Lucas who – perhaps with self-interest in mind – offered a highly positive account suggests drug use in sport was not widely condemned. Regardless of Lucas' subjective posturing, that is the best available evidence and anything else is mere speculation. But discourses and truth are separate entities: Lucas pushed a discourse of validity; later historians have, with anti-doping in mind, reconstructed the story and presented an alternative discourse.

The marathon of four years later, in the 1908 London Games, produced a controversy which some historians have taken to be doping-related. The Italian runner, Dorando Pietri, was leading the race in the final stretch when he fell over several times with exhaustion. Sensing the Italian deserved to win, officials and spectators helped him to his feet. He was first through the tape in dramatic fashion much to the crowd's pleasure but disqualified and the race awarded to the unpopular American Johnny Hayes. It has been claimed that Pietri had been doped with strychnine (Hoberman 1992) though the source of such accusations has never been transparent. It is also unclear if it would be considered morally wrong in the early twentieth century.

Some contemporary sources do offer more insight. It was reported in the press that Pietri had fallen four times in the final three hundred yards, and that 'three times after the doctors had poured stimulants down his throat he was dragged to his feet, and finally was pushed across the line with one man at his back and another holding him by the arm' (*New York Times*, 25 July 1908). These two men seem to be Maxwell Andrews and Dr Bulger. The former has left a written testimony of the events of that day:

> As Dorando reached the track, he staggered, and after a few yards, fell. I kept would-be helpers at bay, but Dr Bulger went to his assistance. I warned him that this would entail disqualification, but he replied that although I was in charge of the race, I must obey him. Each time that Dorando fell, I had to hold his legs whilst the Doctor massaged him to keep his heart beating. Each time that he arose, we kept our arms in position behind (not touching him) to prevent him falling on his head, and as he reached the tape he fell back on our arms. Dr Bulger told me that Dorando had taken a dope of strychnine and atropia, and only his attention both on the track and in the dressing room, saved his life. One of my cycling stewards (still living) saw him take the dope on the far side of Wormwood Scrubbs. Lord Desborough (Referee) on receiving the objection from the Americans, asked for my opinion, and I simply said, 'disqualification'.
>
> (Andrews undated)

Rather than being criticised or castigated, Pietri was honoured with a prize apart from the usual medals, essentially in recognition of his efforts. Queen Alexandra presented him with a silver gilded cup, a gesture apparently proposed by the famous author Arthur Conan Doyle who was at the race. Pietri went on to a brief period of celebrity. If there was a drugs issue at the time, it did not seem to concern de Coubertin, who wrote:

> The disqualification of Dorando Pietri, winner of the marathon, infuriated popular opinion. No one can dispute the fact that Dorando was the moral winner of the competition, or that, technically, he could be disqualified. He made it to the Stadium; he did not reach the finish line. He was supported because he was falling down. Whatever the cause of his repeated fainting – a problem with his food intake or the emotions caused by the welcome of the crowd – it deprived him of the means to forge on ahead to the finish line on his own. The thing is, who can deny that in a race of over forty kilometres, failing at the finish line is nearly the equivalent of victory? That is how the English saw it, and the exquisite gesture of their gracious sovereign merely spoke for the unanimous sentiment of the nation.
>
> (1908, cited in Müller 2000: 417–8)

The Pietri case is really interesting but we remain only partially informed. If he took drugs or was given some medical assistance, it did not seem to worry too many people at the time. The Americans argued, quite rightly, that being supported over the line meant disqualification. If drugs were involved in this story, it would be wrong to conclude from a late twentieth century perspective that it was hypocritical to make an informal award to Pietri.

The issue of inhaling extra oxygen – essentially an artificial introduction of a natural substance – provoked some strong criticism in 1908. Jabez Wolffe was a British long distance swimmer who took part in the highly competitive quest to swim the English Channel, though after 22 attempts between 1906 and 1913 he never actually made a successful crossing. During the swim he was given doses of extra oxygen, though it is not clear how this was administered. His rival, Montague Holbien (who also was unsuccessful in his attempts), described this form of enhancement as 'unsportsmanlike'. This was supported by the British aristocrat and sportsman Lord Lonsdale who argued that 'the use of oxygen is unsportsmanlike and un-English' (*New York Times*, 4 October 1908). Lonsdale here draws from the idealistic notion that the English as a 'race' approached sport with a strong sense of morality and fair play. In this vision, sport should be about doing the best given natural limits, and about enjoying the spirit of fair competition. It should certainly not involve taking drugs or any sort of artificial enhancement in order to boost performance. However, Dr Leonard Hill, a physiologist who had conducted experiments on oxygen and performance, contested this point. He argued that oxygen should be seen as no different to other forms of sustenance such as food. However he does suggest strongly that sport was far from a level playing field:

> Almost the whole of modern sport is conducted with artificial aids. The record feats of today are too often not sport, but deadly, earnest business. Either, I say, limit sport to reasonable feats of endurance or else add oxygen to the other artificial aids now employed in breaking records, and so diminish the harm done to the athlete's body.
>
> (*New York Times*, 4 October 1908)

In his analysis of the situation, Hill contends that it is sport itself that places the pressure on the body, and that drugs and other nutritional aids actually serve to protect athletes from that form of pressure.

Drugs in society

Interest in drug use and application needs to be seen in the context of two countervailing forces. First, a new discipline of the body that focused on the problem of fatigue and had grand designs of social reform and modernising zeal. Second, a temperance movement that had focused on the social and physical problems associated with alcohol but then turned attention to other drugs by the end of the century. It is interesting that both had better health and better societies as their overarching principles. When a drug might be seen as a stimulant it would be praised for its help in resolving fatigue but if it was abused and became associated with vice or crime it would attract criticism. In other words, often it was not the drug itself that was really the issue, but how it was being (ab)used and by whom.

It can be argued that both sport and stimulant drugs are derived from the anti-fatigue movement of the mid-nineteenth century. Anson Rabinbach has argued that from the 1870s onwards fatigue was seen by scientists, writers, industrialists, and political activists as 'the chief sign of the body's refusal to bend to the disciplines of modern society' (1992: 38). Whether at home or in the colonies, European middle classes sought to transform those considered slothful, indolent, weak or ineffective:

> The discovery and diagnosis of fatigue generated a proliferation of efforts to chart its course, find its cure, or at least modify its effects. Such efforts were joined not only by physiologists, but by social hygienists, engineers, psychologists, and social reformers for whom fatigue represented the threshold of human limitation; the barrier that society should strive to bring under control of medicine, technology, and politics. Underlying the anxiety and hostility that surrounded fatigue was the utopian ideal of transcending it. The result would be not only a vast release of the latent energies of society but a productivist civilization, resistant to moral decay and disorder. Behind the scientific and philosophical treatises on fatigue lurked the daydream of the late nineteenth-century middle-classes – a body without fatigue.
>
> (Rabinbach 1992: 44)

The modernisation of sport was arguably an attempt to rationalise and discipline societies using structured physical activities. Team sports in particular were the products of urban, industrial societies, sponsored by factory owners to keep workers healthy, and encouraged by governments as a more acceptable leisure time activity than drinking alcohol. The late Victorians transformed working-class sport with a view to making it more rational, orderly, less violent and more socially acceptable (Holt 1992). In Europe and America religious organisations used sport as a means of channelling the energies of young people. And in the colonies, sport was a means of disciplining the indigenous people, improving their health so they could help improve their societies. Sport represented Western modernity. As Michael Anthony Budd has written on the cult of the strongmen in the early twentieth century:

> The image of the physical cultural strongman supported claims of European superiority and pointed to the complexity of bodily desires that fuelled capitalist consumerism. Physical culture discourse and iconography thus vividly evoke the body politics of industry and empire in their articulation of the possibility of actual physical transformation.
>
> (1997: ix)

It was understandable that, if scientists were interested in revitalising forms of stimulants such as coca or strychnine, athletes who sought success through good health would also use them. The ideology of modernity and progress that was linked to industrial productivity and the rationalising impulses of European and American cultures provided a backdrop to the development of drug use in sport. However, sport's supposed health and community benefits, more likely to be seen at lower levels of competition, would lead to an anti-doping ideology.

The countervailing trend came from religious and temperance movements anxious about the problematic effects of addiction, abuse, misbehaviour, decadence and degeneracy. This can be seen from the earliest discourse on coca leaves. The Spanish conquistadors thought chewing them was a 'vice' and were critical of their function in 'native' 'heathen' rituals (Berridge 1999: 216). The German natural scientist Poppig argued in 1835, after spending five years with 'natives' in the Peruvian Andes, that Europeans could not use coca without suffering health consequences and addiction. He recounted tales of Europeans going insane after over-consumption (Christison 1876).

American temperance campaigners were drawing attention to the misuse of drugs in society. In 1879 a public meeting in Massachusetts focused on 'concern over the health and moral problems created by the escalating use of habit-forming drugs and alcohol' (Goodwin 1999: 23). Such events were part of a middle-class reactionary movement based on religious values and anxiety over the state of the country's moral and physical health. All manner of accusations were made. In 1883, campaigners worried about opium being used by factory owners to combat workers' fatigue, and that shipping companies 'supplied coca leaves to increase the endurance and loyalty of stevedores on the New Orleans docks' (Goodwin 1999: 32). Around that time, activists claimed that addiction to opium and other drugs such as laudanum were more widespread than most people would believe. And even shop owners were under the spotlight: it was reported that 'drug store soda fountains laced other drinks with opium or cocaine to habituate young people to their establishments' (Goodwin 1999: 44).

By the late nineteenth century narcotics such as opium were treated like alcohol: as leading inevitably towards a life of vice and crime. Cocaine became associated with prostitutes and crime among working-class African Americans in the southern states. Heroin, cocaine and opium had been the focus of several legal regulations during the interwar period. In America, the first law limiting cocaine distribution was passed in 1897 in the state of Illinois. In 1906, the drug was officially criminalised in the Pure Food and Drug Act (Andrews and Solomon 1975). The media ran regular stories linking the drug to vice and crime. Prostitutes were said to be addicts, violence and murder fuelled by cocaine highs, especially in the black working-class communities. Thus 'the resentment of criminal and minority users combined with the fear that thousands of impressionable young men were ruining their lives with a cheap and accessible drug' (Courtwright 1995: 213) produced both a public outcry and legal response.

The irony of this connection was that if workers were introduced to cocaine by their employers in New Orleans and other Southern docks, then it was the desire to relieve fatigue in work that contributed to wider addiction and social problems. By 1900 this work-related drug use had spread among the local populations. 'Some saloons in black neighbourhoods had gone out of business because so many of their patrons turned to cocaine. Other saloons exploited the demand by offering the drug for sale on their premises' (Goodwin 1999: 121–2).

On both sides of the Atlantic, drugs were slowly becoming associated with social problems, health issues and addiction. The debate on drugs in sport reflected the debate on drugs in society: an on-going discussion on whether the potential benefits could be controlled and if they outweighed the broader risks. Stimulants in sport were being framed in the same way other drugs were, and Virginia Berridge sums up the changing attitudes to opium and heroin thus, 'the definition of drug taking as a problem – the whole "problem framework" which began hesitantly to emerge in the nineteenth century – remains now as a dominant and usually unquestioned legacy' (1999: 236). As the twentieth century progressed, doping in sport was accompanied by the question of risk and eventually the demands for policy intervention.

Conclusion

There is not a great deal of evidence on drug use in this period. However, it is clear that the myth of the 'golden age' of equal competition based on talent alone does not fit with reality. The examples of alcohol use, coca and kola tonic drinks, oxygen, cocaine and strychnine use all show that some athletes were willing to try stimulant drugs to gain that extra edge over their competitors. Within the context of rationalisation and the disciplines of modernity, it seems that drug use in sport was in part related to discourses of progress and superiority. However, such claims should be treated with caution. There is no evidence of widespread drug use, there were some critical voices, and the wider social receptiveness towards drugs was becoming more cautious by the early twentieth century.

The pitfalls of drug use had been identified: addiction, physical and emotional damage, and social degeneracy. It was clear that sporting role models could not be seen to be drug users. The middle-class prudery and construction of social fears through drugs had made the connection between athleticism and doping extremely tenuous. Despite this, the construction of new knowledge through scientific research continued apace. The modernistic ideal of the human motor, fashioned and improved through surveillance and discipline, found expression in the emerging discipline of exercise physiology. On both sides of the Atlantic, networks of scholars set about trying to find effective 'ergogenic aids' for sport.

3 The science gets serious, 1920–1945

Introduction

The period from the 1920s through to the mid 1940s was a formative time for the development of a rational-scientific approach to sport and to the use of drugs for sport. John Hoberman (1992) offers a useful outline of developments in Germany that deals with some of the complexities. This stands in contrast to the misleadingly narrow perspective that has been offered by some writers (e.g. Houlihan 1999). Such brief accounts refer to the use of amphetamines by the military during the Second World War and the Nazi experiments with steroids around this time. However, this approach locates drug use either with a reviled totalitarian regime or with the highly demanding needs of troops during the war. It offers little understanding of how drugs were treated in terms of ethics or health. Neither does it discuss how the science of doping developed as a genuine, open and legitimate source of research-based knowledge.

This chapter addresses these questions by drawing on comparative national examples. Sport was becoming increasingly scientific from the early 1920s, leading to a raft of experiments on potential stimulants. As such, this was a hugely important period for understanding how drugs became part of sports culture linked directly to the science of performance. Much of the research was conducted in the USA and Germany, as the science communities sought to develop new knowledge, not least after the lessons of the First World War. Governments and scientists realised that war was becoming more technologically focused, and that scientific research would have wider applications. German research in drugs and sport began in the early 1920s, American work soon followed. By the 1930s and 1940s, physiologists were offering summaries of the research that would explicitly direct athletes to the more useful substances. As the military demanded knowledge on stimulant drugs for combating fatigue in war situations, sports-related research of the 1920s and 1930s would underpin further inquiries into amphetamines and other drugs. By the 1940s, British scientists joined the quest for good information on the applications of drugs in physically stressful situations. The consequences were significant: sports doping after the war resulted from the value placed on amphetamines by wartime researchers, and the dissemination of this new 'wonder drug' to the public. This period was hugely influential in providing information and developing new drugs. The possibility that this was a form of cheating was hardly ever mentioned and certainly did not hold up scientific research or athletes' usage.

Training, science and the road to doping

During the period from the turn of the century to the early 1920s, the application of scientific ideas to sports coaching went through an important transformation. Some elite athletes turned to dedicated coaches in their attempt to optimise their performance through training. There had been some training in earlier periods, but the underlying assumptions of what could be achieved altered dramatically. Early manuals on coaching had advised that athletes possessed a natural, fixed, innate level of physical ability (Beamish and Ritchie 2005). This correlated with the physiologists' view of the body: that it might be refined through harmony with nature and repetition, but that it could not be enhanced. Such ideas were not restricted to sports. In the field of industrial relations, tasks were reorganised so that greater efficiency could be achieved. The Taylorist approach to work assumed a worker could only do a set amount of labour. The traditional theories of the body worked on the notion of 'fixed capacity':

> Performance improved through increased precision and better technique – not increased performance capacity ... time and motion studies, whether in the workplace or on the track, optimized a given work capacity; they did not try to expand it by developing an untapped 'potential' capacity. Track and field coaches and industrial managers were working from the same set of assumptions about human performance and sought increased efficiencies rather than expanded capacities.
>
> (Beamish and Ritchie 2005: 417)

For example, the French coach Georges Hébert focused on attuning technique to athletes' natural movements while working on an efficient style. A group of Finnish runners benefited from his expertise, including Hannes Kolehmainen who took three gold medals at the 1912 Olympics and Paavo Nurmi who dominated distance events during the 1920s (Beamish and Ritchie 2005: 417). These coaches and athletes operated under a paradigm of 'natural' limits within which only the strategy of conserving energy could lead to higher levels of achievement.

However, by the 1930s, scientific research on human physiology was beginning to show that interval training, resistance training and varying the levels of exercise intensity were among the factors that could contribute to improving performance further. Around the same time, advances in other biological disciplines challenged the notion that the body worked within fixed limits. A new conception of the body had arrived that permitted and indeed promoted 'the continuous, scientifically assisted enhancement of athletes' performance capacities' (Beamish and Ritchie

2005: 428). This ushered in a new era in which the connection between sport and science was formalised in the sub-discipline of exercise physiology and would push forward the possibilities of physical enhancement.

Enhancing performance the American way

The first signs of this new body of science in North America can be seen in the years immediately preceding the First World War. Several textbooks appeared that aimed at providing physiological knowledge based on research and sound scientific principles. Of the four main contenders for 'first' physiology text, three were published in New York and the other in London (McArdle *et al.* 2000: 18). The *American Journal of Physiology* was established in 1898. In 1904 the Nutrition Laboratory at the Carnegie Institute in Washington DC was set up to study nutrition and energy metabolism.

By the 1920s there were physiology labs at George Williams College, the University of Illinois and Springfield College, but the most famous and significant development was the opening of the Harvard Fatigue Laboratory in 1927. Research focused on the nature of fatigue, performance, and how they might be influenced by ergogenic aids. Experiments sought to discover the properties of specific physiological factors, such as the body's adaptability to environmental factors, its response to stresses such as intense exercise, the physiochemical properties and behaviour of blood, and understanding factors relating to fatigue such as altitude, lactic acid and potential stimulants. Thus, the Harvard Laboratory 'pioneered many aspects of exercise physiology ... the discoveries made in the areas of blood chemistry in exercise, aerobic and anaerobic work capacity, diet and physiological adaptation to physical work at altitude would all be used to enhance world-class athletic performance once applied sports physiology had embraced the mid-twentieth century paradigm shift in human performance' (Beamish and Ritchie 2005: 419). The innovative work and international collaborations meant the experimental work 'formed the cornerstone for future research efforts in exercise physiology' and 'influenced a new generation of exercise physiologists worldwide' (McArdle *et al.* 2000: 19–20). Despite a lack of explicit focus on sport there is no doubt the research findings could be translated into the context of exercise, training and dietary supplements.

For instance, D. B. Dill, the science director at Harvard published a paper in 1932 showing that injecting adrenal hormones reduced the sensation of fatigue in subjects undertaking walking tasks (Dill 1932; McArdle *et al.* 2000). It may not be possible to establish a direct causal link, but events within sport clearly show an interest in such innovations. In 1932, a drug called Pelanin was developed by Okamoto after doctors in the Los Angeles Olympics 'observed that some of the best women lost because of menstruation' (Bøje 1939: 465). This led the Danish scientist Ove Bøje to argue that 'it is conceivable that the administration of sex hormones or of preparations of adrenal cortex might increase physical output'. He continued, 'In special cases among women athletes, hormone treatment has been found to be of assistance in attaining the highest level of performance. In particular, the administration of an oestrus-producing substance may delay the onset of menstruation if this should coincide with the date of the contest' (1939: 465).

Many American athletes experimented with ergogenic aids. The Yale University rowing team assumed the edge they had gained over their rivals in the 1920s was down to the application of ultraviolet rays before a race. The same technique was used by Allan Woodring, the 200-metres gold medallist in the 1920 Olympics, and his fellow countryman Jackson Scholz who won the same event in 1924 (Hoberman 1992: 136–7). University rowing crews also tried sugar lumps and peppermints as a stimulant. It was reported in 1926 that Harvard had been experimenting with sugar lumps for two years. Yale University's squad had been advised in 1925 by a doctor to eat a pound of peppermints before a race. Edward Stevens, the coach at Harvard, scoffed at his opponents' naivety, claiming that the only outcome would be cases of nausea (*New York Times*, 30 March 1926). This was something of an international debate. The Harvard/Yale dispute had arisen because the English Cambridge University team had admitted using extra sugar when beating their traditional rivals Oxford in 1926.

All of which may not seem too serious if the only temptations were the almost childlike bag of sugary treats. However, there were instances of 'hard' drug use in cycling in the 1920s. The six-day races held in New York and Chicago attracted audiences of up to 150,000 fans. Local government officials worried that the demand placed on riders left them no choice but to seek sustenance in stimulant drugs. According to one concerned New York politician, they were 'kept in their saddles by resort to drugs' due to the exhausting nature of the competition (*New York Times*, 17 February 1927). Ove Bøje described the incident, 'the participants were so intoxicated with cocaine that their bearing after the race was like that of lunatics' (1939: 457). The sports physician Max Novich (1964) also alleged that interwar cyclists had used cocaine, caffeine and other drugs.

These examples may be episodic and it is difficult to gauge from existing sources how representative they were of wider practice. However, they do demonstrate the tendency among some athletes of the time to innovate for performance enhancement unimpeded by the notion that this might somehow be a form of cheating. Some of the substances used may seem comical to modern readers while others are recognisable in today's lexicon of 'hard' drugs. However, three important cultural dimensions in the history of sports doping can be seen: intention, cultural acceptability, and some sort of scientific knowledge base. This latter point is not always clear cut. Sometimes the science seems far removed from the day-to-day experimentation that took place on athletic tracks, in cycling races, in swimming pools and at rowing events. Indeed, it could be argued that the connection between theory, research and sports practice was tenuous and variable. And yet, scientists played a role in creating publicly available information from which athletes and coaches could derive their ideas.

One such example, Professor Peter Karpovich, physiologist at Springfield College and one of the founding members of the American College of Sports Medicine (in 1954), was one of the leading experts on the subject of drugs in

The outcomes make for fascinating reading. He claimed that alcohol might be useful for warming up but is detrimental to muscular performance even in small doses. Alkalies such as sodium bicarbonate might benefit athletes' performance. The research on ammonium chloride was considered contradictory and its usage was not recommended. Benzedrine, a form of amphetamine, had been the subject of a range of studies that had not offered definitive conclusions (Ivy and Krasno 1941). Karpovich claimed its chemical composition and physiological action were closely related to those of adrenalin. The main benefit was that amphetamine could counteract fatigue but had risky side effects: 'it is a powerful and dangerous drug and its excess may lead to insomnia, hypertonia, and circulatory collapse' (1941: 437). However, he acknowledged that the lack of scientific evidence and these associated risks did not stop it being used, as there had been 'rumours that Benzedrine has been responsible for an improvement in athletic performance' (1941: 437). Caffeine had first been shown useful in experiments by the pioneering Italian Musso in 1893. By 1941, other experiments had confirmed its value for delaying fatigue and increasing work output. Karpovich warned that the consensus of medical opinion was that caffeine should be prohibited to athletes, though he failed to fully explain why. Cocaine had been shown by Musso and some German physiologists to improve performance but he argued it should not be used because of its dangerous and addictive qualities. While this ostensibly reflects a concern for athletes' health, research on side effects had not been undertaken for any of the ergogenic aids under discussion. So to single out cocaine was a leap of logic probably based on wider social fears about addiction and social deviance rather than on clear empirical evidence.

A number of studies reviewed by Karpovich showed the potential for hormones to benefit athletes – this was a vital first step to the development of anabolic steroids and testosterone for sport as these were being introduced into other areas of medicine (Hoberman 2005; see Chapter 5). Physiological effects of hormone use included increased metabolism, adrenalin-induced rise in blood pressure, and greater muscular strength. The earliest studies were by Brown-Sequard (Hoberman 1992) but his findings were dismissed as subjective. Other researchers including D. B. Dill and Okamoto, as noted above, had proved positive effects, which led to Karpovich's conclusion that there 'is sufficient evidence that administration of hormones may raise the level of physical fitness' (1941: 441). No health risks were mentioned, and thus he suggests, with a great deal of prescience, that 'further research in this field will undoubtedly be fruitful' (1941: 441).

Karpovich thought extra oxygen would only be useful for a few minutes at a time. Phosphates might be useful but there was a lack of definite proof. The same was said for sugar and extra vitamins. He really only thought that the value of ultraviolet rays had been supported by experimental research, though even this could be 'psychological'. Therefore this review would lead readers to imagine hormones to be the best way forward for athletic improvement. This was perhaps a reflection of the optimism expressed about hormone treatment for a range of mental and sexual problems since the early twentieth century (Hoberman 2005). It was only four years later that one of the most famous reviews of the potential for hormone use to enhance physical capacity was published: Paul de Kruif's *The Male Hormone* (1945). Therefore, the American situation was characterised by experimentation by athletes and a background of scientific research. The situation in Germany was developing along similar lines.

Arbeitphysiologie: science and drug use in Germany

As discussed in the previous chapter, a number of European scientists had pushed forward knowledge on the effects of certain substances on fatigue and performance before the First World War. The experiments of French physiologist Tissié do not appear to have led to a sustained network of exercise- or sport-related science in that country. There were small collections of researchers in Denmark and Sweden. However, there was a collection of scientists working in Germany on exercise physiology and ergogenic aids. Clinical studies investigated many of the same substances that American physiologists and athletes were interested in. So, it was no accident that such drugs became popular among athletes in Germany.

As with researchers in the USA, physiologists set the context by developing studies on enhancing performance capacities. L. Pikhala (1930) showed that regular training lowered the heart rate required to work at a fixed level. By showing the effects of variations of rest, activity and intensity he 'articulated the essential components of progressive resistance training for athletic development' (Beamish and Ritchie 2005: 418). This research was complemented by E. H. Christensen (1931) who studied the relationship between fitness, workload and the improvement of maximum oxygen carrying capacity ($VO_{2\ MAX}$) as well as the impact of varying resistance and intensity. By the early 1930s there were dedicated journals publishing a range of experimental findings on sport and exercise science.

German researchers were a few years ahead of their American counterparts. One of the first studies of the interwar period with the potential application for drug use in sport was that made by the German physiologist Herbert Herxheimer (1922). Using 46 subjects he aimed to discover the effects of caffeine on their sprinting and cycling performance. The results were mixed. The drug had no effect on their 100-metre times, but did improve work output on a bicycle ergometer task (Williams, 1974: 53). Around this time, stimulant usage was becoming increasingly known in sporting circles. A German medic, Dr Willner, claimed in 1925 that cocaine was widely used at sports events. Athletes also turned to kola nuts and an American product that mixed cocaine with kola nuts had been marketed in Germany under the name of Dallkolat. Ultraviolet rays were popular for their supposed stimulant effect (Hoberman 1992). Thus, science, commerce and a powerful desire for success lay behind the choice and availability of drugs for athletes.

In 1922, Herxheimer claimed that the commercial product Recresal (primary sodium phosphate) would lead to an increase in physical fitness. This was followed up by research published in 1930 by Poppelreuter showing the benefits of Recresal to both mountain climbers and soldiers. Poppelreuter had conducted some self-experimentation, taking Recresal himself every day for several years.

He reported feeling physically and mentally healthy while taking this drug. The research had differing results: some studies showed a reduction in fatigue, while others showed that phosphates only had a placebo effect (Hoberman 1992). All of which led Ove Bøje to conclude that they cause 'a purely subjective feeling of freshness and zest for exertion ... none of the investigations ... allow the definite conclusion that phosphates increase the standard of athletic achievement' (1939: 445–6).

Bøje flagged up the extent to which athletes were disinclined to wait for scientific confirmation and were more easily persuaded by simple publicity than by science. He noted that 'phosphates are in great demand in athletic circles, particularly in Germany, owing to intensive advertising of their beneficial properties' (1939: 446). Demand for such stimulants was recognised by other scientists at the time. Herxheimer claimed that with 'the approach of the sports season ... the aspiring athlete will need his full dose of phosphates' (cited in Hoberman 1992: 134). It is revealing to see the social processes at work here. A drug which has no clear basis in science was advertised and sold for its stimulant properties, was taken by athletes desperate for that extra edge, even though the health risks remained unknown. Indeed, Bøje was concerned that over-indulgence would have potential (though unspecified) ill effects.

The most outspoken anti-doping critic in Germany was Professor Dr Otto Reisser, Director of the Pharmacological Institute of the University of Breslau (Hoberman 1992). In 1930 he reviewed a range of potentially useful substances for enhancing performance, concluding that the few of some value were phosphates, caffeine, theobromine and chocolate (Reisser 1930). He maintained that the physiological complexion of the athlete could not be manipulated by such straightforward processes as adding new substances to their diet. This is an important point, though he was not representative of the wider scientific community. To argue that the human body was too intricate to be simply 'adjusted' by one drug or another ran contrary to the blossoming science of doping. He was also aware that athletes had a one-dimensional view of performance and stimulants. They would ignore scientific advice in their quest for the holy grail of performance enhancement. With that in mind, he addressed the German Swimming Federation in 1933 with the following admonition:

> The use of artificial means [to improve performance] has long been considered wholly incompatible with the spirit of sport and has therefore been condemned. Nevertheless, we all know that this rule is continually being broken, and that sportive competitions are often more a matter of doping than of training. It is highly regrettable that those who are in charge of supervising sport seem to lack the energy for the campaign against this evil, and that a lax, and fateful, attitude is spreading. Nor are the physicians without blame for this state of affairs, in part on account of their ignorance, and in part because they are prescribing strong drugs for the purpose of doping which are not available to athletes without prescriptions.
>
> (Reisser 1933: 393–4; cited in Hoberman 1992: 131)

This commentary is fascinating for a number of reasons. The notion that some sort of consensus had been formed around the use of stimulants in sport is somewhat presumptuous given the lack of other similar comments to be found around this time. Certainly his idea that the 'spirit of sport' has been transgressed does not reflect other scientific writings or the behaviour of some athletes. His claim that usage was widespread may be correct. But to claim that the results of competitions revolve around doping more than anything else was an exaggeration. He indulged in some hyperbole when arguing that this is an 'evil' and it is 'spreading'. He then goes on to blame sports governing bodies and physicians for their role in the problem. However, it is unlikely that highly motivated athletes will turn away from any form of assistance if their will to succeed is powerful enough. More than this, interest in drug use for sport was being actively promoted by scientists on both sides of the Atlantic. These comments were somewhat out of place given the advances and interests of human physiologists on both sides of the Atlantic. They were in many ways a signal of things to come. This may be the first time doping was referred to as an 'evil', a word that was applied much more regularly as anti-doping policy and science got underway in the 1960s (see Chapter 6). Moreover, this idea that all athletes should be under suspicion pre-empts later anti-doping fanaticism that cast blanket generalisations over certain sports, certain countries and certain groups of athletes.

Other German research was developing alongside the demand for drugs in sport. In 1930, Graf conducted an experiment on subjects riding bicycles. They were given either chocolate on its own, combined with caffeine, or combined with cola nuts. He found that the cola was more effective than the caffeine, raising work output between 20 and 30 per cent (Karpovich 1941: 437). In 1930, Theil and Essing published research showing that subjects' work capacity on a bicycle ergometer increased following the use of cocaine. The following year, a study was made of cocaine by Herbst and Schellenberg, showing that it helped increase the speed of recovery after riding stationary bikes (Karpovich 1941: 438). It is perhaps unsurprising that athletes showed an interest in cocaine and seem to have used it. In his survey of international sport, Bøje offers the opinion that 'it is not an easy matter to determine to what extent cocaine is resorted to by athletes; but no one acquainted with the position would gainsay that they are far from ignorant of its uses' (1939: 457). Nothing suggests German athletes were any different, and if their compatriot physiologists published research showing the performance-enhancing benefits of the drug, anecdotal knowledge would find support in clinical research.

Other drugs were discussed in the literature. Poppelreuter made the assumption that 'nerve poisons' such as strychnine, alcohol, caffeine, cocaine and arsenic would act as performance-enhancing agents (Hoberman 1992: 134–5). Lehman and colleagues (1939) showed 'that amphetamine enabled greater work ability in tests to exhaustion on a bicycle ergometer' (Williams 1974: 37). By the early 1940s, various groups of German scientists had conducted tests with ultraviolet light rays on subjects in running, swimming, rowing, cycling and using an ergograph, all of which indicated 'a beneficial effect or irradiation upon muscular performance and general well being' (Karpovich 1941: 446).

There were a number of research groups in Germany interested in making a stronger connection between performance sport and drugs. There is some evidence that this was reflected 'on the ground'. As such, John Hoberman's summary seems apt, 'sports medical and physiological journals of this interwar period make it clear that the use of drugs in German sport was now widespread and widely known' (1992: 134). Sport was becoming modernised, the application of sport was central to that process, and Germany was one of the leading lights.

Pep pills and monkey glands: doping in interwar Britain

The American and German situations showed how science informed doping, that exercise physiology offered empirical and clinical knowledge about the types of drugs used by athletes. The sub-discipline was less developed in Britain during the interwar period, and we can only speculate whether studies in other countries had any impact. If any culture retained that idealisation of the golden era of amateur-gentlemen functioning entirely on natural talent, it would be found in the British middle and upper classes. Although a fictional account, the Oscar-winning film *Chariots of Fire* shows the contrast between this culture and the modernising influence of the American coach Sam Mussabini, focusing on the British competitors at the 1924 Olympics. Amateurism certainly was a powerful force in British sport which articulated specific values and shunned others. Sport was something to be approached with honest endeavour and modesty: it was a pleasant distraction, rather than a career or a status symbol.

Indeed, the clash of cultural values, or at least of national circumstances, was illustrated by the English runner Jack Crump in 1937. While in Germany at a race meeting, his team-mate Powell had sought advice from a local doctor on his Achilles injury. Powell 'returned to the track just in time for the start, but also in possession of some tablets which the doctor had given him'. Crump immediately became suspicious, 'I insisted upon him giving me the tablets, which I suspected were some sort of "dope", and destroyed them'. Powell had recovered well enough from his Achilles problem to finish second in the 800 metres. When he went back to the same doctor for further treatment the next day 'he was asked if he had taken the tablets'. Upon saying no he had not, 'he was told that had he done so he would have finished first not second', leading Crump to reflect, 'thus doping would appear to be no new phenomenon in sport' (1966: 54).

Perhaps paradoxically, one of the most honest accounts of 'pep pill' use during this (and perhaps any other) period came from a British source. Leslie Knighton was manager of Arsenal in 1925 when he doped his players with pep pills obtained from a local doctor. Although Knighton did not know what the pep pills contained it is likely from the side effects described that they were amphetamines, a drug which was used by medics in the 1920s before gaining wider popularity in the 1930s. As a means of representing oneself in such an affair, Knighton deserves some sort of prize for unashamed honesty. The section of his autobiography detailing the episode was titled 'I Dope Arsenal for a Cup Tie' (1948: 73). The background to the affair is fascinating and the re-telling somewhat colourful.

Knighton was in a state of anxiety over his team's confidence and they had been drawn in the FA Cup against fellow Londoners and city rivals, the physically intimidating West Ham United. He was alone in his office 'with my head in my hands, wondering how on earth we could make sure of putting West Ham out of the Cup' when he was visited by a 'distinguished West End doctor'. Unsure what to expect, the manager invited him in and offered a cigarette. The doctor explained his purpose:

> I'm a keen Arsenal fan, Mr Knighton. I trust that you will not be offended if I say that we have shown some unhappy symptoms, and have a rather poor chance of survival after meeting West Ham?

The doctor, it transpired, was a regular at home games. He continued:

> What the boys require is something in the nature of a courage-pill. Occasionally, we administer such things to patients requiring abnormal stamina or resistance for a particular purpose. They do no harm, but simply tone up the nerve reflexes to produce the maximum effort, and they leave no serious after-effects.
>
> (Knighton 1948: 74)

The manager saw nothing wrong in this proposal, viewing the pills as similar to any other form of tonic designed to give the players 'hearts as big as bullocks'. He was reassured about the health risks, and asked the doctor to keep this confidential as he was unsure about public reaction if the story leaked out. This is an important point: although he did not refuse the pills, Knighton knew that the media and public would be critical of his attempts to gain some advantage in this way.

The match was away, at Upton Park, and Knighton had discussed the plan with the players, promising to take a pill himself, 'as a sign of good faith'. An hour before the game they sat together and each swallowed their 'silver pill' with a glass of water. 'Just before kick-off time I saw that the boys were getting restless. So was I. I felt I needed to run, jump, shout. There was something in those pills. I felt I could push down a wall with my fist' (Knighton 1948: 75). All of which was unfortunate as the referee called off the game due to thick fog, 'Getting the boys back to Highbury that afternoon was like trying to drive a flock of lively young lions' (Knighton 1948: 75). And it left a painfully dry, bitter thirst (dehydration is a classic symptom of amphetamine use) that Knighton failed to quench with numerous large glasses of water.

The replay was scheduled for the following Monday. Once again, the manager joined the players to take the pills, and again the fixture was postponed by fog. Once more 'we had to undergo those agonies of thirst and violent restlessness. I felt I could have knocked [Primo] Carnera for six – but what was the good of that!' (Knighton 1948: 76). When the match was at last played, the pep pills had the desired effect. After surviving the West Ham early onslaught, the Arsenal team 'seemed like giants suddenly supercharged', they 'tore away with the ball, and put in shots that looked like leather thunderbolts'. They dominated the second half, 'ran like Olympic sprinters behind the ball, jumped like rockets to reach the high ones, and crashed in shots from all angles and distances'. West Ham had 'no defence against the pluck-pills' (Knighton 1948: 76). The game ended goalless. The replay was at Highbury. However, on the day of that match the players refused to take the pills because of the raging thirst it left them with, 'when the players saw the little red box in my hand, the yell that went up nearly split the roof' (1948: 77).

After drawing 2–2, Knighton wished for the pills, 'Our play was not nearly so determined as it had been in the former game, and I believe we should have netted two more goals if the pills had been taken' (1948: 77). At the fifth attempt the fixture was settled in favour of West Ham after the Arsenal players again refused the pills. Knighton reflected on his missed opportunity, 'I often wondered if we should have won if the boys had been doped for that game. Just a bit of extra pep when we were so often pressing the West Ham defence ... We did not lose when we took the pills, and did not win when we rejected them. I wonder?' (1948: 77).

This is a fascinating episode. It reveals the potential for medical experts to persuade coaches and managers about the value of drugs without providing them with full information about what the drugs are and what effect they would have. The temptation of the extra edge is obvious and Knighton was left with some regrets at what might have been. Like Jack Powell's experience in Germany, the doctor told the Arsenal manager that 'those pills would have taken us to Wembley' (1948: 77). There was little sense in his mind that this was a form of cheating. It has been claimed that Knighton's confession in 1948 and the discussion of this event in 'matter-of-fact' terms by the amateur international footballer Bernard Joy in 1952 shows that even as late as the early 1950s doping was not seen as 'cheating', 'improper' or 'reprehensible' (Waddington 2000: 99). And yet, Knighton's unwillingness to publicise his ventures at the time do suggest a much more complex situation in which risks were taken by people in authority knowing full well that bad publicity and criticism would follow if the story were to leak out.

Another example from English football did become public knowledge, perhaps because it was not about chemical drugs but the use of gland extracts to improve strength, speed and stamina (this was a process similar to isolating hormones). This technique was first used by Wolverhampton Wanderers in the late 1930s under the guidance of manager Major Frank Buckley who had sought specialist advice from Menzies Sharpe (it is unclear from available sources if Sharpe was a qualified doctor or some sort of alternative health guru). Unlike Knighton, Buckley was willing to inform other clubs and the media of his use of this treatment, denying that it was a form of doping because it was not harmful (*News of the World*, 26 February 1939). This logic reflects that of physiologists who only imagined the ethical problem to be health, not fair play.

The treatment was assumed to be responsible for the improved success rate and physical strength of Buckley's team, leading other club managers to approach Sharpe for the treatment. Portsmouth's manager Jack Tinn put his players on it for the rest of the season. But Sharpe was vehement in his claims this was not a quick fix stimulant and managers should not imagine a 'swift course of gland treatment would get them promotion this season!' (*News of the World*, 26 February 1939). Nonetheless, a partial explanation was offered to readers of the *News of the World* which claimed every bodily movement was governed by 'various glands'. If a footballer was showing signs of slowness it was – apparently – because the 'gland governing the combination of thought and action is not up to scratch, and the brain's message to the legs takes a fraction of a second longer than normal to get through' (*News of the World*, 26 February 1939). By identifying the misfiring gland Sharpe could inject an extract from the suprarenal cortex to remedy the fault thus reviving the player's speed, quickness of thought and improve his overall action.

Fulham, Preston and Tottenham had joined Wolves and Portsmouth in the ranks of gland extract enthusiasts. Tom Whittaker, a trainer who had worked with Arsenal and the England teams in football and tennis, was sceptical about the true effects of gland treatment. Having undertaken some experimental research he argued in a *News of the World* article that while it may help in cases of illness, it would have 'no useful effect on normal healthy players' (Whittaker 1938).

Whittaker also discussed some of the other stimulants used in sport, including the 'new drug, Benzedrine':

> This has the effect of pepping-up sluggish players and may succeed in rousing the spirit of men and women who are only at their best when they are on the verge of losing their tempers. It is stronger than aspirin and caffeine, and brings about a reaction afterwards, although it is not the type of drug to which one becomes addicted. Instead, one is inclined to get fed up with it. I regard it as dangerous in the long run.
>
> (Whittaker 1938)

This is clearly some attempt to balance up the relative merits and costs of stimulants. However, Whittaker is convinced that while such practices may lead to 'performances of unbelievable brilliance' the threat is to health and to the very foundation of sporting values. 'But at what a cost of human suffering! That would be the end of sport as we understand it.' Just to firm up Whittaker's fears, and make it a sensation, the article was headlined, 'Will Science Give Us ROBOT ATHLETES?' (Whittaker 1938). There was a sense of danger here, that science and sport were leading humanity towards something insufferable. The notion of playing with humanity itself was clearly something that vexed journalists and readers. The Football League clubs certainly did not like the idea of gland treatment, though perhaps they were more concerned at the sportsmanship issues than the over-dramatic implications of the newspapers. There was speculation that the Football League would try to stop clubs using gland treatment when it met in June

1939 though this early anti-doping initiative did not seem to get far (*News of the World*, 7 May 1939). By the end of the season, Wolves had finished second in the League and lost the FA Cup final to fellow gland users Portsmouth. It was a passing fashion, but gland extract therapy revealed something of the diverse attitudes to doping in British sport. It also prompted a response from Ove Bøje:

> Quite recently, the newspapers announced that the remarkable performances of the Wolverhampton Wanderers football team were due to gland extract treatment provided for the players by their manager, Major Buckley. The Portsmouth team consequently decided to follow their example. Such cases show that, nowadays, no hesitation is felt in administering even *hormone* treatment as a method of improving athletic performance. I do not know what hormones the English footballers use to score their goals, but this, presumably, is irrelevant, as we are probably dealing with a purely subjective phenomenon.
>
> (1939: 464–5)

So by the end of the 1930s we can see a stark contrast between cultural situations. Also, there was something quite incoherent and fragmented about the science and sport relationship. The next major steps towards doping knowledge and application would happen during the years of the Second World War.

Amphetamines and the war

It was largely in the field of military medical research that experiments into fatigue and stimulants were being pushed forward in the 1940s. By that stage, of course, the world had become politically divided and scientists were conscious of how their research might be applied in practice. The potential of amphetamine was of interest to Allied and Axis powers, with Americans and Germans building on previous work in the field. What had started out as a generic interest in human capability developed into a hugely important race that might help soldiers, pilots and other personnel improve their contribution to the war.

Peter Karpovich worked with a colleague from the University of Wisconsin, F. A. Hellebrandt, to produce a paper in 1941 for the journal *War Medicine* that summarised research on 'methods used for improving the physical performance of man'. This drew similarities in fatigue patterns in 'sport, labour and military training' taking the lessons learnt from athletics to the field of warfare, 'the history of competitive athletics and the longevity of sportsmen suggest that strength, skill and efficiency can be increased significantly without detriment to the machinery of the human body' (1941: 746). However, the usual caveats expressed in sporting contexts about damaging long- and short-term health were set aside, 'the principle does not hold when applied to life and death exhaustion problems associated with the pursuit of war' (1941: 748). This is an important point, because it shows the requirements of war partially removed the brakes of ethics and health in sport when researching stimulants. Thus, Hellebrandt and Karpovich wrote:

Small doses of alcohol, beverages containing caffeine, amphetamine or coca leaves all raise the levels of physical performance in the course of prolonged effort by lessening the appreciation of fatigue. They may thus be classed as emergency remedies which improve staying power and work capacity, even if muscular strength is not increased.

(1941: 764)

In the context of warfare, research aimed to push the boundaries of performance without being overly inhibited by ethical concerns, and facilitated the dissemination of exercise physiology-based knowledge on stimulant drugs. Ove Bøje's important review article was not published in a sports journal but appeared in the *Bulletin of the Health Organisation of the League of Nations* in 1939. Two years later, Ivy and Krasno (1941) produced a review of the pharmacological literature on amphetamine sulphate (Benzedrine) for *War Medicine*. At the same time, sports journals continued to publish research on these issues. Foltz, Ivy and Barborka's study of caffeine and recovery from fatigue appeared in the *American Journal of Physiology* in 1942. And in 1946, Haldi and Wrynn published an experiment in the *Research Quarterly for the American Physical Education Association* which tested the benefits of metrazol, Benzedrine and caffeine on swimmers. Moreover, the public dissemination of knowledge made research on amphetamines for warfare available in summary form to any potential user. A 1942 report in the *New York Times* summarised research by Dr Maurice Tainter, Professor of Pharmacology at Stanford University which was presented to the Society of Experimental Biology and Medicine. He claimed that one-ten-thousandth of an ounce of methyl-benzedrine (a derivate of Benzedrine) 'would keep a man so stimulated and alert that sleep would be impossible for at least eighteen hours', he would 'think more clearly and react faster' (24 December 1942). This public debate was linked directly to the research competition between the Allies and Axis powers: the article was titled 'Pep Pills Keep Users Awake 18 Hours: Drug Reputedly Used to Spur Hitler's Troops'.

The American scientists Ivy and Krasno added further commendations:

Amphetamine in most persons certainly promotes wakefulness and the feeling of well-being and decreases the sense of fatigue and boredom in performing tedious work over rather long periods. The drug tends to improve psychomotor activities in the majority of subjects.

(1941: 41)

The potential downsides were very much an after-thought. The researchers warned of the 'habit-forming potentialities' of amphetamine and that its impact on complex task achievement was unknown, but suggested more research to establish whether it were any better than caffeine for stimulating mind and body.

A number of exercise-specific studies had also raised the profile of amphetamine and caffeine as performance stimulants. Foltz *et al.* (1942) found that caffeine increased work output of subjects pedalling a bicycle ergometer for 4 or 5 minutes. Benzedrine was found to retard the onset of fatigue (Alles and Feigen 1942, cited in Haldi and Wrynn 1946), and to increase the work output in a cycling ergometer experiment (Knoefel 1943, cited in Haldi and Wrynn 1946). Meanwhile, Haldi and Wrynn (1946) found that metrazol, Benzedrine and caffeine did not improve speed in swimming a 100-yard sprint, arguing that such stimulants hence seemed more useful for longer forms of exercise. There seemed to be openness across international boundaries here: Alles and Feigen, and Knoefel, were Germans whose work was cited in American studies. The academic community were at least continuing the practice of sharing information, though the political context was at odds with such generosity.

The benefits of amphetamine were discussed in the *British Journal of Addiction* precisely because of the supposed benefits they provided to soldiers and pilots. In a Special Issue of the journal which included a range of articles such as 'Amphetamine in the Air Force' by Professor R. C. Browne, a number of contributors reflected upon the commonly held ideas about the drug. According to Browne, the Royal Air Force began researching this question in 1940 under the auspices of its Flying Personnel Research Committee after a German pilot who had been shot down had been found to have had a small amount of amphetamine with him (Browne 1947: 64). After testing the drug on British pilots during their actual flight operations, it was found that it prevented fatigue, did not deteriorate performance, but neither did it help achieve markedly improved results. Apparently, the pilots did not 'like being doped' and saw drugs as a 'phoney' method of enhancing their mental and physical abilities (Browne 1947: 70). This is another indication of British anxieties over doping or unnatural forms of enhancement, and given the tradition of sport in the military probably not too far removed from anxieties over sports doping.

A more positive slant was taken by other authors who argued that the military did in fact give it to their forces:

> It reduces bodily fatigue and allows the tired individual to carry on for a longer period. This ability to stand strain longer was of value in the war. More than seventy-two million tablets of Benzedrine were issued to the British Forces and a greater number to the American.
>
> (Rudolf 1947: 71)

The manufacturers of Benzedrine claimed the drug increased endurance, quickened reaction times, and produced an overall sense of well-being. Its everyday usage extended to all social classes. The British doctor H. Crichton-Miller used the drug for over 10 years, for mental exertion activities such as speech making, and physical activities such as mountain climbing. He agreed with the claims made for the drug (1947: 46).

The examples from the Special Issue were focused on military activity and not published until after the war, probably for reasons of national security. A similar position was taken on work by two physiologists at the Institute of Physiology, University of Glasgow, D. P. Cuthbertson and J. A. C. Knox. The research was commissioned by the Military Personnel Research Committee of the Medical Research Council in 1942 and facilitated by the Director of Hygiene at the War Office. The study addressed the following:

> First, did analeptics [central nervous stimulants] really increase the output of work of fatigued men, and, if so, what dosage was required? Secondly, would the analeptics keep tired men awake and able to perform their duties satisfactorily? And thirdly, if the drugs did have these effects, what was the cost to the organism? That is, was the burst of energy accompanied by untoward symptoms and was it followed by a dangerous 'flop'?
>
> (1947: 42)

The experiments were conducted in 1942, clearly a vital year in the war, and were 'wanted quickly' by the Council. They must have been used secretly as the full publication did not come until five years later in the *Journal of Physiology*. The drugs tested were Benzedrine and methedrine – noted as the same substance being used during the war by the Germans under the name of Pervitin. The conclusions were highly positive. It was claimed that tests using hand and cycle ergometers and in the field showed the drugs 'increased the subject's capacity to sustain a given level of work performance' for around an hour at a time (1947: 57). Methedrine had 'diminished the fatigue and discomfort of a long route march' and Benzedrine led to 'increased wakefulness in fatigued men under the conditions of a military exercise' (1947: 57–8). There was no marked 'flop'. Moreover, while a few 'unfavourable signs' showed on the men, dosage levels of 10 mg of methedrine or 15 mg of Benzedrine were 'found to be safe and effective' (1947: 58). Higher dosages would however lead to 'overdose'. However, they did note another British study had shown that up to 125 mg of Benzedrine given regularly over a 'long period' resulted in 'no evidence of physiological damage' (1947: 56). Clearly, this sort of research had tested the levels of amphetamine usage with a view to finding the optimum dosage for performance and health.

This was a vital time for the growth in knowledge on doping products. The war created a fundamentally different environment: no longer was the *ad hoc* nature of interwar research good enough. Applications were a matter of national security and perhaps even survival. As the next chapter shows, the impact would be profound.

Conclusion

The interwar period was a time of substantial changes that set the framework for later developments in sports doping. By the 1940s there was an emerging science of amphetamines that would radically alter the landscape of doping in post-war sport. Also, by this stage the clinical research, media discussions and the athletes' rumour mill were becoming increasingly internationalised. Within the space of two decades doping had progressed from something localised, experimental and unsystematic to a subject with its own body of scientific knowledge, experts, networks of interested parties, and an emerging debate that reflected anxieties over health in particular.

There were some concerns in international sporting circles however. In 1938, after meeting in Warsaw, the IOC included the following response to questions on doping: 'The use of drugs or artificial stimulants of any kind must be condemned most strongly, and everyone who accepts or offers dope, no matter in what form, should not be allowed to participate in amateur meetings or in the Olympic Games' (IOC 1938: 30). Given the evidence presented in this chapter about the range of drug use in North America and Europe, this was an insipid response. The IOC must have been aware of drug taking but failed to offer a discussion, definition, set of penalties, or any indication of how this ruling might be policed. Moreover, the idea that all amateur meetings came under the remit of the IOC was clearly not going to sit easily with the national governing bodies in specific countries who felt they were in charge. Without a process of consultation, this statement was never going to be taken seriously.

Science was central to the development of doping, and the focus of subnational networks in the USA and Germany shows how these operated. The British experience differed in that fewer examples of physiological research can be found, but nonetheless the doctor who offered Leslie Knighton the pep pills and the gland extract guru Menzies Sharpe represent the scientific community working with sports coaches to find stimulants and other performance-enhancing strategies. In other cases, the link between scientific research and actual practice is less distinct. Research on the effect of certain drugs went on inside university laboratories and it remains unclear how this disseminated down to practitioners. Nonetheless, we can point to the parallel development in the USA and Germany of research-based knowledge and doping in practice. And many of the laboratory studies were explicitly aimed at discovering the relationship of drugs and performance. As Peter Karpovich showed, the process by which a drug was introduced, experimented with by athletes, experimented upon by scientists and turned into commercially available products by entrepreneurs, was often a cyclical and contingent affair. It is interesting that even in the interwar period, once a drug became widely used some individuals stepped forward to offer critical appraisals of either its health side effects, usefulness for performance or impact on the nature of sport itself. Fashions changed quickly: what seemed to be cutting edge at one time soon became passé because it became common. Seeking that extra something to beat one's competitors would mean finding a drug first – athletes could not wait for scientists to tell them if it was useful or healthy.

The subject of amphetamine use was bolstered by wartime research which allowed researchers to override the usual cautions about health. By the 1940s the drug was being consumed by the public and this led directly to post-war usage for a range of reasons including competitive sports. In later years, a certain divergence would occur: athletes would test the performance limits with less concern for health; doctors would claim that any dosage level would be both damaging to health and unsportsmanlike.

4   Amphetamines and post-war sport, 1945–1976

Introduction

Previous historical accounts have underplayed the impact of the Second World War on doping in sports. The immediate post-war relief and austerity would not have engendered concerns about using the sorts of stimulant drugs that had helped soldiers and pilots. Health issues about drugs were not foremost in the minds of a public readjusting to normal civilian life. At the same time, international sport was being relaunched: the Olympics were held in 1948 in a euphoric but under-prepared London. Drugs were simply not an issue. However, amphetamines had been widely used during the war, were sold as medicines to the public, and so were gradually introduced into sport. The way in which this happened meant that the drugs were not immediately perceived as a problem, a threat to sport, as undermining fair play, or as creating a significant health issue.

Within the space of ten years the situation had altered dramatically. The Olympic movement was better organised but becoming overrun by the politics of the Cold War: the USSR entered the Games in 1952 and quickly locked horns with the USA for supremacy. Evidence shows that amphetamine use was widespread in the USA and Europe.[1] By 1957 the American Medical Association (AMA) was so concerned about this practice that it publicly condemned it, linked it to wider social problems of drug addiction and set up a dedicated Commission to further investigate the social and scientific questions. Elsewhere, doping was an open secret in cycling, seen by many as a necessary adjunct to training for the extreme demands of the sport. The deaths of two cyclists in major international competitions – Knud Enemark Jensen at the 1960 Olympic Games and Tommy Simpson during the 1967 Tour de France – were high profile and blamed on amphetamines. In the wider social context, the media and policy makers were increasingly seeing these types of drugs as a problem as they became inextricably connected with social degeneracy, crime and drug counter-cultures. However, even after testing for amphetamines was introduced in the mid 1960s, and steroids became more widely available as an alternative from the late 1960s, use of the drugs continued. The clash of cultural values between different sports led to the IOC's anti-doping response, based on amateurism and fair play.

An affront to amateurism: doping in the Olympics

The first evidence of drugs being used in sport after the war comes from a medical doctor attending the 1948 London Olympics who also saw that cyclists in and out of the Games were using what he considered to be illicit means of performance enhancement. Dr Christopher Woodward was an official advisor to the British team in 1948 and made his concerns public through a letter to *Cycling* magazine that was picked up as a story by the *New York Times*. He wrote:

> I became suspicious that some competitors were receiving artificial stimulants at the Olympic Games. Two or three weeks later I was able to see things at closer range at the world cycling championships at Amsterdam, where I spent some of my time on the inside of the track. Few other than our own team knew who I was. Imagine my surprise, therefore when a garrulous foreigner surreptitiously tried to show me his pet concoction of strychnine, caffeine and Benzedrine ... [drug use in sport] is more widespread than people think ... I've just visited Sweden and people there told me it was going on constantly.
>
> (*New York Times*, 1 October 1948)

It is not clear if such anxieties had much impact on the athletes of the 1952 Olympic Games in Helsinki. Reports are contradictory on this question. The United States weightlifting coach, Bob Hoffman, accused the Soviets of using testosterone, 'I know they're taking the hormone stuff to increase their strength' (cited in Todd 1987: 93). The Austrian sports medic and prominent anti-doping expert Ludwig Prokop (1975) found syringes in the locker room of speed skaters during the Winter Games of that year though it is unclear what was in them.

However, suggestions of doping were countered by Dr Arthur H. Steinhaus, Professor of Physiology at George Williams College, Chicago, who had been a medical expert at the Games. He claimed that science had helped athletes alongside better coaching and training, but strenuously denied that stimulants such as Benzedrine, pervetin and caffeine were being used in athletics, 'There's no place for that kind of stuff in athletics. And besides, I doubt if any known stimulant would really help a man win a race' (*New York Times*, 2 August 1952).

After the 1960 Rome Olympics the British runner Gordon Pirie revealed that the problem of drugs in sport was a 'serious problem' that 'springs mainly from the extreme nationalism now poisoning sport' (1961: 29). He witnessed athletes using Benzedrine at the Games, he was offered pep pills in the British changing room by a 'well known doctor', and another doctor responded to his abstinence by saying, 'You must be one of the few mugs left who doesn't' (1961: 29). This is a remarkable anecdote of collusion in the ranks of British team medics suggesting that doping was known about and sanctioned by figures in authority.

Pirie widened the scope of his criticisms, 'I believe it is standard practice before a race in certain Iron Curtain countries. Sudden staggering performances quite out of keeping with known form can only be explained by the use of drugs, and I believe their frequent use has accounted for the short athletic careers of some fine performances' (1961: 28–9). Certainly we can see that if the popular rumours highlight doping as standard practice among opponents, an athlete could easily be considered a 'mug' not to take stimulants when offered.

It was at the Rome Games that one of the most (in)famous tragedies took place. In the searing temperatures of the Italian summer (it was reportedly around 40 degrees Celsius), Knud Enemark Jensen and two of his Danish team-mates were hospitalised with heat exhaustion after a cycling race. Sadly, Jensen died, his life a brief testament to sporting dedication. It has frequently been claimed that amphetamine use played a key role in this story (see Møller 2005 for a critique of the flawed scholarship on this incident). The wider context of drug use in professional cycling certainly shows that amphetamines were used by cyclists (Wheatcroft 2003). Moreover, the Dutch cycling federation chairman, Piet van Dijk, said of those Games that 'dope – whole cartloads – were used in such royal quantities' (Woodland 2003: 108). The Danish team doctor did admit giving his riders a drug called Ronical which is a vasodilator. However, Ludwig Prokop later claimed that the autopsy performed by Italian doctors on Jensen revealed traces of amphetamine. In fact, the autopsy has never been made public and the Danish sporting authorities investigated the matter in conjunction with the Italian doctors and saw no reason to pursue any punishments (Møller 2005).

While the evidence of usage has never been proven, Jensen's posthumous reputation continues to be sullied by those eager to use his body as proof of the health risks of doping, and by those whose retrospective accounts neatly see his death as the catalyst for an international anti-doping movement. As Møller (2005) so convincingly shows, myths have been taken for facts in this case. Such has been the power of this myth that it has been repeated by various academics, sports administrators and writers of popular sports history. Perhaps it is even more important to realise that anti-doping and cycling leaders have succumbed to this myth. One of Prokop's principal allies in the anti-doping fight of the 1960s was Belgian doctor Albert Dirix, who was inspired by the idea that Jensen died due to a drug overdose:

> We doctors wish to prevent such tragedies as those which occurred at the Rome Olympics, in which a cyclist died and two of his companions became gravely ill as a result of doping; for us it is a matter of conscience and nothing can be more criminal than to destroy the health or the life of a young athlete.
>
> (1966: 185)

Such was Dirix's commitment that he described doping as an 'evil' that had 'assumed such large proportions ... that it seems absolutely essential to fight against it with every possible weapon' (1966: 183). But the legacy of the Jensen myth continued. In 1976, Wlodzimierz Golebiewski, the then Vice-President of the International Amateur Cycling Federation, claimed in reference to Jensen that, 'This young man had taken a large overdose of drugs, which had been the cause of his death' (cited in Woodland 2003: 108). Prince Alexandre de Merode, head of the IOC Medical Commission from 1967–2000, wrote in an official IOC book that 'according to the experts' reports, [Jensen] had taken a strong dose of amphetamines and a nicotine acid derivative, administered, rumour had it, by his coach' (1999: 8). The lack of facts gave way to speculation, Golebiewski continued, 'No one has ever proved whether he took the overdose himself or whether the drug was administered by someone else without his knowledge' (cited in Woodland 2003: 108).

If cycling was seen as the 'problem' sport of the Olympics, the Jensen myth helped those who wanted to focus attention on one specific group of athletes. An additional facet was the history of professionalism in cycling, which many in the Olympic movement saw as undermining the amateur rules and spirit of the Games. In 1969, an Indian doctor G. M. Oza argued the case that doping was linked to 'artificial' forms of enhancement and thus to professionalism. His vision of sport saw the athlete 'struggle, strive and sweat for success ... real sportsmanship is associated with natural potentialities' (1969: 210). This meant that, artificial aids such as doping were seen as 'unnatural and contrary to the spirit of the Olympic Games' (1969: 210). Thus, the use of popular drugs such as amphetamines continued to be a thorn in the side of Olympic fanatics through the 1960s and into the 1970s. As we shall see, anti-doping was strengthened by the IOC's commitment to the cause, while steroids became the major issue of the 1970s. However, the distinct cultural frame of Olympism constructed doping and anti-doping as a fight for the heart of humanity itself:

> I would prefer to class the athletes as a 'better race' on the surface of the earth. The future generations would inherit their characters and therefore a continuity of good society would be maintained. I would never wish then, that we should be deprived of such fine, healthy persons as a result of doping. Even if the history of doping dates back to the beginning of human civilization, I feel that it is not in keeping with the Olympic ideals and with the present time. The 20th century is for co-operation and not for unfair competition. The Olympic symbol is for developing sporting friendship between the different civilizations of the world.
>
> (Oza 1969: 212)

This is the epitome of the sporting idealism model. Oza does not just put athletes on a pedestal, he practically has them as demi-gods. Not for him, the more cynical view of George Orwell that sport is war minus the bullets nor Bertold Brecht's opinion that 'Great sport begins where good health ends' (cited in Hoberman 1992: 1). But Oza was so in keeping with the IOC's idealism that two years later he was allowed the opportunity to continue his anti-doping, pro-sport fanaticism in the *Olympic Review*. In this second piece he wrote:

> Olympism hates the use of drugs in sport ... It is better to die a natural death and end life in a characteristic sporting manner than to collapse after having become a drug addict. The [Olympic ideal], one of the noblest in the world, is threatened with extinction ... I appeal to the legion of Olympic lovers

residing throughout the world to do their utmost to preserve the dignity of the Olympic Games. We have pledged to have an anti-doping crusade with a view to safeguarding the moral and physical health of our athletes. This is the only measure which will protect 'strength, health and purity' – the aims of sport.

(Oza 1971: 179–180)

Couched in religious vocabulary, Oza imagines a crusade against the heresy that threatens the virtuous demi-gods. The symbolic importance of doping went beyond Olympism, to sport and to universal morality. However, the Olympics were a focal point and amateurism was a peg on which to hang all manner of issues.

Doping in European sport

European athletes seemed to be increasingly turning to artificial aids despite the fantasies of Olympic virtue being preached in IOC publications, and promoted by both anti-doping scientists and national media.

In 1950 it was alleged that the Danish rowing team had been given drugs to help them win the European Championships and this had led to some of them collapsing at the end of the race. Their team doctor, Dr Axel Mathiesens, had provided them with a substance called Androstin over a 12-day period leading up to the race. Mathiesens had a good reputation as a former rower and thirty years' experience as a medic. This incident provoked a vigorous debate on the doctor's behaviour. Fellow Dane, Ove Bøje considered enhancements such as nutritious foods and ultraviolet light to be forms of doping, but other sports administrators disagreed with his assessment. There was no consensus on what constituted doping, what should be the law against it, and therefore no set of punishments for 'offenders' (Mullegg and Montandon 1951). In other words, the policy and medical elements had yet to be sorted out.

This was the first case in which the media began to take the role as moral arbitrators, with some journalists making as much of a story from it as possible. A medical problem had become a public issue, the newspapers could sniff a scandal, and the pressure was on the authorities to respond as quickly as possible. While the sports federations and doctors deliberated over the case, the media saw a story and ran with it. There was a more accusatory tone to the media's interest than had been the case, for instance, with the gland therapy episodes in English football in 1939. A new discourse of doping-as-scandal was in its infancy in Europe.

By the time of the successful ascent of Everest in 1953 – using extra oxygen – athletes such as the renowned, soon to be the first sub-four-minute miler, Roger Bannister, were applying this to sport. He told the conference of the BASM, 'While breathing the ambient fresh air, signs of fatigue make their appearance about the 7th or 8th minute afterwards as against only 22 or 23 minutes after the taking of oxygen' (*Bulletin du Comité International Olympique* 1954). The oxygen debate was blurred by the fact that oxygen is a naturally occurring substance. It was probably also clear that regulation through a ban or a test would be ridiculous.

This was a precursor of the debate which began in the 1960s on whether altitude training constitutes a form of doping-related cheating.

Outside the Olympics and power sports such as weightlifting and bodybuilding, the issue of doping surfaced in football. A set of tests on Italian footballers in 1961 showed 36 per cent had taken amphetamines before games (CoE 1964). A year later it was reported in the British press that the lower league football club, Cheltenham Town, had been given pep pills by their manager, who claimed, 'These pills give the lads extra energy in the last twenty minutes of the game. I don't think it's unfair. It's open to anyone to buy them at the chemists, as I did' (*Daily Mail*, 10 September 1962).

In one of the first examples of the British media turning drug taking into a scandal – a sign of changing attitudes – the *Sunday People* journalist Michael Gibbert exposed the practice of amphetamine use among Everton players in the 1961–2 season and during their championship-winning season of 1962–3. Players took the drug Driamyl, popularly known as Purple Hearts, and Benzedrine, before games for performance and recreationally at parties in the evening after games. Gibbert's 'most serious' claim is that the drugs 'were made freely available, by certain club officials, to anyone in the team who wanted them. These officials actually supplied and distributed the drugs before matches and even during training sessions' (*Sunday People*, 13 September 1964). The goalkeeper at that time, Albert Dunlop, came forward as the key witness, explaining that the club trainers handed out the pills during training and an hour before matches. The players would take up to four pills before big games, and sometimes – as during their 4–0 win over Chelsea – 'literally ran the opposition into the ground' (*Sunday People*, 13 September 1964). The story was given a further edge of seriousness by the fact that Dunlop ended up addicted to the drugs and to alcohol which led to him being dropped by Everton and eventually hospitalised. Not only were the drugs a form of cheating, but they could lead to serious physical and mental health problems.

The club's board members issued a statement that denied any complicity in the drug use, but did admit some mild stimulant drugs had been used by players 'entirely as a matter of personal choice, and medically, we are told, these pills, in the quantities taken, could not possibly have had any harmful effect on any player' (*The Times*, 12 September 1964). This shows the acceptance of everyday use of amphetamines and a belief they were harmless. Perhaps this was the last time a professional sports club in Britain publicly acknowledged and even condoned the use of stimulant drugs. But the lurid headlines continued as other newspapers tracked down the supplier of Everton's drugs (*Daily Herald*, 14 September 1964), and the doping issue was linked to an investigation that the club tried to bribe opponents to fix match results (*Sunday Telegraph*, 13 September 1964). The media were beginning to show a greater interest in this subject, and it was perhaps a shock to Everton's administration that they would be under the spotlight for such activities. This is perhaps best explained by reference to the changing relationship of football and the media. The 1960s generation of top stars such as George Best flaunted the wealth they received after the end of the maximum wage and the rise of endorsement commercialism. They had become like pop stars whose private lives were making newspaper headlines. Drugs were becoming a social issue in Britain and footballers were under pressure to be 'clean' role models.

More explicit use of drugs was to be found in European professional cycling. In September 1949 a cyclist died of 'amphetamine poisoning' in a hospital in the Italian city of Rapallo (Venerando 1964: 48). The famous Italian rider Fausto Coppi, who won several titles including the doubles of the Giro d'Italia and the Tour de France in both 1949 and 1952, later admitted using amphetamines. After his retirement he was asked if riders took them and replied, 'Yes, and those who say otherwise aren't worth talking to about cycling'. And of his own usage, he said, 'Yes, whenever it was needed' which was 'practically all the time' (Wheatcroft 2003: 207–8).

In 1955, Frenchman Jean Malléjac zigzagged across the road then collapsed during the Tour de France while beginning the climb up Mont Ventoux. After lying unconscious for over 15 minutes, he was revived by Tour doctor Pierre Dumas, with the stimulant solucamphre. The rider lashed out and had to be tied down for his own safety. Dumas described his shock, 'It chilled my blood' (cited in Fotheringham 2003: 161). The physical effects suggested overuse of amphetamines leading Dumas to try and persuade team doctors to exercise more caution when distributing medical products to cyclists.

Such incidents hinted at a wider pattern of usage that was broadly accepted by cyclists and their advisors. The historian of professional cycling, Geoffrey Nicholson, has argued that until the mid 1960s most people involved in the sport saw the 'sensible use of stimulants' as unproblematic, it was known to exist but seldom mentioned in public forums such as the press or other publications (1978: 90). Dumas was confronted by uninformed yet popular drug habits which included using amphetamines, coca, strychnine, solucamphre and morphine. This was done quite openly, with riders sharing needles and sometimes injecting themselves during races. They would often call for a bottle of drug-based stimulant drink just before the final stages of a race. Dumas said 'the cyclists took everything they were offered. It didn't matter what they took, as long as they believed in it' (cited in Fotheringham 2003: 158).

During the 1959 Tour de France, he intercepted a package of strychnine addressed to one of the teams. In 1960, the French national team manager during the Tour, Marcel Bidot, commented that, 'Three-quarters of the riders are doped. I am well placed to know since I visit their rooms each evening during the Tour. I always leave frightened after these visits' (cited in Woodland 1980: 41). That same year, Dumas found the eventual winner of the Tour Gastone Nencini 'lying in his bed with a drip infusing primitive hormones into both arms – and smoking a cigarette' (Fotheringham 2003: 160). During the Tour, French rider Roger Rivière broke his back after crashing into a ravine. He never cycled again. He was a well-known drug user and admitted using a 'massive' dose of amphetamines in 1959 when he broke the record for the one-hour race (Fotheringham 2003: 142).

In 1961, police raided the cyclists' rooms during races in Belgium, Switzerland and France (Novich 1964: 272). In an article for the Dutch newspaper *De Telegraaf*, in 1961, the veteran cyclist Wout Wagtmans described the context of drug taking:

> You hear the name of some product or other somewhere and you go and buy it. If it doesn't help, you take more or you try something else. When I talk to young riders now, they are always interested in drugs. The result is that one minute they're really flying and a day later they're nowhere.
>
> (cited in Woodland 1980: 24).

Gordon Pirie, the British runner, observed that, 'I believe in international cycling many of the competitors are "souped up" to a dangerous degree' (1961: 29). It seemed that even the high profile incidents were not putting cyclists off their drugs.

In 1963, Ludwig Prokop attended the Tour d'Autriche where he 'found the sweatshirts of a number of Austrian cyclists padded with large quantities of amphetamines and other stimulants' (1975: 86). Two years later, a Dutch cyclist whom Prokop tested positive for a 'massive use of amphetamine' was disqualified and sent home where he was feted as a 'hero and a martyr and I as the controlling physician severely defamed' (1975: 86). This showed the antipathy, if not outright opposition, towards the process of drug testing on the part of cyclists and their supporters. Another example of this came in 1964. It seems that efforts to control doping in the 100-kilometre Olympic race were not accepted by the cyclists despite what had seemed to happen in the 1960 Olympic race. The supervising physician Albert Dirix wrote in 1988 that he and Dumas set up the 'control' but the 'task remained incomplete due to a boycott' (1988: 669).

As medical attempts to stop doping grew throughout the 1960s so did evidence of drug use. In the first event to have urine tests for amphetamine use, the Tour of Britain in 1965, three Spanish riders and one English were found to have used the drug. A series of tests of Belgian cyclists showed that 37 per cent of professionals and 23 per cent of amateurs had used them (Donohoe and Johnson 1986: 6). However, one of the most trenchant and public debates around drug use came in the mid 1960s when five-times Tour de France champion (including four successive victories) Jacques Anquetil decided that honesty was better than hypocrisy. In 1965 he declared, 'Everyone in cycling dopes himself. Those who claim they don't are liars' and 'We could do without them in a race, but then we would pedal 15 miles an hour instead of 25' (Scott 1971). In that same year, French doctor Paul Chailley-Bert told a conference that over 1,000 cyclists had died as a result of amphetamine use (cited in Woodland 2003: 113). Although it is unclear how he came to this figure, it must be taken as a sincere effort to gauge the impact of the drug over a long period of time.

Events seemed to be bearing out Chailley-Bert's pessimism. Two riders, André Bayssière and Charles Grosskost, collapsed during the Tour de l'Avenir in July 1965 (the shorter amateur race run alongside the Tour de France), both of whom admitted taking amphetamines. A year later in the Tour, Dutch pair Lucien Aimar and Arie Den Hartog suffered in a similar way though they did not confess to any wrongdoing. Drugs were banned in cycling in June 1966, and Dumas said at the time, 'As far as I'm concerned, this isn't funny any more' (cited in Fotheringham 2003: 163). The open secret of experimentation was fast becoming a more serious social problem.

As will be discussed in Chapter 7, the attempts to ban doping in cycling at this time were met with resistance and derision. Going into the 1967 Tour, the Englishman Tommy Simpson continued his habit of taking amphetamines and when he reached the Mont Ventoux stage added large gulps of brandy to his pills. He had secured a supply of Tonedron, seen as the Rolls-Royce of amphetamines and much better than the common Benzedrine. He spent £800, a large amount of money for a cyclist in the late 1960s. He had a reputation for drug taking, and for trying to find any sort of enhancement that would help him achieve success. Testimonies from those close to him at the time reveal the day to day habits of pill taking and securing supplies from Italy. He would justify this by arguing the medical benefits, that they relieved the pressure placed on his body by the long rides of up to 280 kilometres a day (Fotheringham 2003). Like previous riders whose mind and body gave way, Simpson's ill health was seen in his random zig-zagging across the road on Mont Ventoux. He staggered along for a while, fell off, got back on, then collapsed at the side of the road. Pierre Dumas was on hand, and worked to revive him, but he died on the way to the hospital. Simpson's death was obviously a tragic combination of drugs and the extreme pressures of the Tour. Yet, the construction of a memorial to Simpson on Mont Ventoux suggests that many fans of the sport remember him as a hero not as a dope villain or a cheat.

Arguably the aftermath of Simpson's death was to force cyclists' drug habits into a murky, secretive world and made the cycling community close ranks on the issue. Anquetil was gradually marginalised for his radical position. Testing was no longer protested against. But cyclists came up with more imaginative ways to avoid a positive result, for instance, by having a pre-prepared urine sample hidden on their body so that it would appear they were giving a genuine sample (Voet 2001). Suspicions still accompanied most of the riders in the 1970s (Woodland 1980). Thus, one of the most concentrated and regular places where doping occurred went under a process of change as anti-doping had to be accepted.

From high school to pro sports in America

For post-war athletes and coaches, the potential for wealth, status and national prestige was such that health issues (for some, at least) were secondary concerns to be managed appropriately but not to disrupt the route to personal glory. As Max Novich told the joint meeting of the IOC and the International Congress of Sports Science in 1964:

> Following the return of the veteran to college, the use of amphetamine 'pep pills' became quite common among professional and intercollegiate athletes.

Since the high school athlete and coach are influenced by the professional and intercollegiate athlete, the amphetamines became popular even in interscholastic athletics.

(1964: 272)

In the wider social environment, amphetamines were becoming more commonly used for a range of ailments. For instance, by the mid 1950s there were at least eight different types of inhaler on the market in America that used forms of amphetamine such as Benzedrine. In his history of the drug, Scott Lukas writes:

> amphetamine or the 'pep pill' was commonly used by the forces during World War II. Several hundred million tablets were supplied to troops on both sides. At the end of the war many soldiers returning home spread the news about this invigorating drug. In the 1950s college students, athletes, truck drivers and housewives, in addition to soldiers, were using amphetamine for non-medical purposes ... use of the drug expanded in various countries during this decade, as production of amphetamine increased significantly. It was being marketed to treat obesity, narcolepsy, hyperkinesis, and depression, but people were taking it primarily to increase energy, decrease the need for sleep, and elevate mood.

(Lukas 1985: 16–17)

These aspects of the history of doping have been underappreciated in previous studies. Amphetamines were not simply seen as a 'doping' substance at this time but an acceptable and legitimate public medicine. Therefore, it is important to gain some sense of historical change and contingency and not simply assume that anyone using the drug in sports at this time can be called a cheat.

High school and college sport has, unlike in Europe, been a highly competitive arena in America, where careers can be made or lost. Teams at this level have been given high levels of support from their local community, thus bringing financial rewards and social status to players and managers. One of the leading British anti-doping campaigners of later decades, Sir Arthur Gold, argued that it was indeed in America in the 1950s that 'the abuse of drugs in sport began on a substantial basis'. He put this in context:

> sport was largely in the hands of the universities and high schools and the coaches, who are rather like football [soccer] managers but even less secure, were usually employed on a one year contract. A successful team, and they were re-employed – an unsuccessful team and they joined the dole [jobless benefits] queue, if they had the equivalent of one, and since most of their competitors were virtually in the same position as their employees, and were expendable, they didn't hesitate to introduce drug abuse into sport in the USA.

(Gold 1986: 3)

The situation in America was becoming a matter of public concern by the late 1950s. So much so that the most important medical organisation in the country began to take the matter seriously. The AMA brought amphetamine use in sport to the attention of the world's press, commissioned further research, and focused on the potentially harmful effects of using such stimulants for sport. In doing so, they significantly altered the nature and scope of the debate, and set the framework for a new body of social and scientific knowledge to emerge that explicitly aimed – for the first time – at a critical assessment of doping. This mirrored similar initiatives around the same time in Italy that focused on cycling and football (see Chapter 6).

During the Association's conference in June 1957, Dr Herbert Berger, a consultant to the United States Public Health Service and expert on drug addiction, claimed that amphetamines were being widely and indiscriminately used by athletes and coaches across the USA. Berger admitted that it could have a powerful effect on performance but stressed the 'violent, rapacious and criminal behaviour' that resulted from using the drug. He denounced its use in sport in emotive terms, as 'shocking and vicious' (*The Times*, 6 June 1957). The sports most affected were considered to be boxing, American football at both professional and college level, and high school athletes. Berger even strongly hinted that the drugs helped those runners who had broken the four-minute mile, first achieved by Roger Bannister on 6 May 1954. However, these claims were strongly denied by athletes (*The Times*, 6 June 1957). The following day saw further denials, such as that by Ron Delany, who took gold in the 1500 metres in the 1956 Melbourne Games:

> The whole idea that drugs are being used is absurd and crazy. I have never used drugs to help me run and I don't know of anyone else who has, anywhere in the world. That includes all the four-minute milers. Track and field is an amateur sport – a clean sport. I don't think anyone in it would want to pay such a price just to win a race or break a record.
>
> (*New York Times*, 7 June 1957)

The drug manufacturers were not content to sit idly back and watch this debate unfold without them. A spokesman for an unnamed company argued that, 'Clinical experience of more than 20 years has conclusively demonstrated that amphetamine sulphate is one of the safest drugs available to medical practice' (*The Times*, 7 June 1957). The medical benefits of amphetamines were considered at this time to be valid and varied and they were almost as widely used as aspirin. So what had prompted Berger's outburst? He admitted that the worst emotional consequences related to those individuals who were already 'high-pitched'. However, his fears were related to broader drug use in society, 'Drug addicts might get their start in taking amphetamines during high school and college athletics' (*The Times*, 6 June 1957). This is an important point for distinguishing the motivations and origins of anti-doping. His concerns were really about addiction and social disorder, not about sports. Therefore, there is at least one trend in anti-doping that focused on what we might call community health, rather than on fair play or the health of elite athletes. As with other drugs, the actual outcomes were exaggerated, and referred to situations of extreme and widespread abuses.

However, follow-up media investigations did uncover patterns of usage and thus presented a wider image of episodic abuse to the public. A high school coach from Oklahoma admitted giving his student athletes phosphate pills, and claimed other high school teams used them. Two American football players admitted using Benzedrine pills while playing for a team in Toronto in 1955, but the club had no involvement or knowledge of their doping habits. Dr Fred Davies, team doctor for the Ottawa Rough Riders American football team argued that the top four Canadian teams gave pep pills to their players before and during matches (*New York Times*, 8 June 1957). In the course of these revelations, the supposedly clean, amateur, Olympics were not spared the publicity. Judy Joy Davies, former Olympic swimmer, was reported to say, 'Some of our champion swimmers fearlessly admit they take pep pills to help them shatter records'. And Neville Scott, an athlete from New Zealand, said 'it seemed certain some Olympic athletes were taking drugs' in the 1956 Games (*New York Times*, 8 June 1957). The media had found that evidence of isolated episodes was enough to support the 'scandal' and scaremongering of the doping threat.

Other sources show that amphetamine use was an everyday occurrence even in youth-level competitions. In 1958, the use of amphetamines by young boxers aged 14–18 at the New York Police Athletic League was so publicly known that the Daitz Research Fund studied their effect. It was found they improved performance in the early rounds but led to higher levels of tiredness in later rounds (Novich 1964: 274). The contested nature of this issue is clear: sports authorities and the media took up a hard line, while evidence of usage shows that many saw these drugs as relatively harmless additions to nutritional preparation at all levels of sport.

One outcome from the AMA conference was a resolution to 'investigate the frequency of the indiscriminate use of such agents, particularly in relation to athletic programmes, and to take appropriate action ... to prevent such abuse' (*The Times*, 6 June 1957). The AMA appointed a Committee on Amphetamines and Athletes and two forms of knowledge gathering were proposed: a social survey on usage and a scientific study of amphetamine's properties. For the social survey, 733 questionnaires were sent to college students, requesting information on amphetamine use. The returns showed that less than 1 per cent admitted any knowledge of the use of the drug during athletic performance. The figure might have been low because of the 'wider type of population' that was consulted (Raynes 1969: 148). A survey conducted in 1958 by the American College of Sports Medicine (ACSM) had focused on a smaller sample of the population: 441 were sent a questionnaire and 133 provided a response; these were 'trainers, coaches and physicians' working in sports (Raynes 1969: 148). Of this response group, 35 per cent had knowledge that amphetamines and its derivates were being used in sport, of which 63 per cent believed these drugs did improve performance (Raynes 1969: 148).

The AMA also commissioned clinical studies on the impact of amphetamine use on performance (for full details see Pierson 1971). When the initial results were announced in May 1959 – that the drug might improve results by as much as 4 per cent – the Association admitted that, 'there is little evidence that pep pills are widely used in American high schools and colleges or in other countries' (*New York Times*, 28 May 1959). This is curious as the ACSM survey and the media reports suggested otherwise; and it is surprising that the AMA made such a fuss over amphetamines only to backtrack on their speculations. In what proved to be worse news for anti-doping, the clinical findings showing that amphetamines could raise performance by 4 per cent, were reported in sensational terms by the media, leaving Max Novich to fear that the 'myth' of enhancement would be 'difficult to dispel' (1964: 274). The British runner Gordon Pirie observed that drug use was widespread in American track and field sport, 'Pep pills are a standard treatment before big races and the pressure put on athletes to succeed at all costs makes such abuses almost inevitable' (1961: 205). So the AMA's pronouncements and research had done little, if anything, to stop the tide of doping; they may even have encouraged some athletes to experiment.

Further studies contradicted the 4 per cent claim, leading to a series of argumentative articles (Pierson 1971). As a result, the positive appraisal of amphetamine as a performance enhancer was replaced by a much more cautious stance. Aware of the conflicting research, the chances that athletes' usage would increase on the basis of scientific confirmation of their efficacy, and the increasing fears in society as a whole about drug addiction, the euphoria had gone. As the British scientist Raynes told the BASM in 1967:

> the general agreement at the present time is, that if amphetamine causes an improvement in an athlete's time of performance, and under suitable circumstances it will, then its effect is a psychological one causing the sense of 'fatigue' to be dampened down and allowing, therefore, the individual to approach nearer to his furthest limit of performance. In no way does it cause any improvement in physiological mechanisms.
>
> (1969: 159)

Perhaps inevitably, this turnaround in scientific opinion had no impact on the users. The former United States Olympic team doctor Robert Voy argued 'during the 1960s and 1970s, amphetamines appeared to be epidemic among professional football teams' (1988: 660). This was brought to the attention of the American public through media articles and personal testimony showing the collusion of staff in schools and clubs:

> Because of the increasing public exposure about the use of additive drugs, most athletes now [in 1971] have to secure them on what could be termed the athletic black market. However, this was not always the case. These drugs were first widely introduced into the American athletic scene by coaches, trainers and team physicians in the high school, college and professional

ranks. Rick Sortun, a college football star at the University of Washington in the early sixties and a six-year veteran of the NFL, has told me about how an assistant coach at Washington used to slip the players 'bennies' surreptitiously before each game.

(Scott 1971)

Max Novich claimed that 'the incidence of usage of amphetamines in athletics is greater than is being reported or acknowledged' (1964: 275). As an example, in the mid 1960s a New York Jets player admitted he 'used to get so high on bennies for the games on Sunday he was still unable to sleep two nights later before the team reported for Tuesday's practice' (Scott 1971). Even by the late 1960s, college students continued to regularly use drugs for sport even if the official sanctioning of this practice, and the source of supply, had changed, as a college Professor acknowledged:

Most college coaches are not slipping their players bennies today, but they are turning their heads while the players use amphetamines secured from the campus drugs scene. A survey, done by a football player at the University of California for a class I was teaching there two years ago, showed that more than 50 per cent of the players on the Cal football team were regularly using amphetamines for games and practice.

(Scott 1971)

Further evidence was brought to light by journalists:

At Stanford, a starting player on the 1971 Rose Bowl championship team has talked about how he and many of his teammates were using amphetamines not only for games, but also for daily practice sessions. And a former middle-linebacker for the University of Southern California, Steve McConnell, told me that the use of amphetamines for games and practice was at least as common at USC as at Stanford and Cal.

(Scott 1971)

Other sports were far from immune from such problems. In 1970 testing began at the World Weightlifting Championships when they were held in Columbus, Ohio. The result was that nine of the top 12 were disqualified when urine tests showed they had taken amphetamines. International weightlifter Ken Patera admitted using them, called the testing ridiculous, and said they had been taking them routinely for years.

One of the most public scandals to hit American sport came in the mid 1970s when Arnold J. Mandell, a psychiatrist working with the football team the San Diego Chargers, made a series of startling revelations about amphetamine use. He was known to the team as 'benny boy' on account of his role as supplier of 'bennies'. Although this practice had been banned by the National Football League (NFL) since 1971, Mandell continued to operate until he was caught in

1974. Accused of supplying 1,750 pills (5 mg to 15 mg each) over a three-month period, including 400 pills each to two players, he decided to speak out and reveal the extent of drug use in football. In 1976 he published a book called *The Nightmare Season* and ended up being reprimanded by the California Board of Medical Quality Assurance for writing excessive prescriptions. Mandell was a highly qualified scientist, a recognised expert on neurochemistry and author of numerous papers and books, as well as the founding chairman of the Department of Psychiatry at San Diego (Donohoe and Johnson 1986). Such was the widespread expectation that drugs would be available that team doctors became embroiled in doping and ran into personal and career problems.

The American situation differs from that of the European sports or the international forum of the Olympics. There was none of the obvious deaths or near-deaths that were worrying doctors associated with professional cycling in Europe. Investigations into amphetamine use seem to have faltered after the AMA's initial momentum faded. Professional athletes seem to have been driven from a young age, and with drugs on relatively easy supply, that usage continued through the 1970s. In fact, the absence of clear ideological agendas – as seen with the Olympics – clear policies and rules, and systematic testing, mean that American sport was arguably more 'open' to doping than other sectors of international sport.

Conclusion

Between 1948 and the early 1970s amphetamine was the most commonly used drug in sports. That is not to say other drugs were absent; athletes turned to caffeine and cocaine as well. As will be shown in the next chapter, it was amphetamine that focused early efforts towards anti-doping science, policy and educational reform. Steroids did not appear until the late 1950s and were not widely used until the mid 1960s.

The history of amphetamine research shows how sport was informed by other social processes, in this case the need for stimulant drugs during the Second World War. For around three decades from the 1930s to the 1960s, amphetamine and its derivatives were broadly assumed to be useful and safe stimulants that could be used (moderately) for a range of tasks that required physical and mental alertness. The nature and culture of international sport changed dramatically during this time. The Olympic movement became more successful and provided a platform for nationalist rivalries and representation. Professional sports began to take more advantage of commercialism, players' wages rose, and the potential for individual sponsorship offered much larger rewards to those who became successful.

The process by which science, warfare and sport became more closely connected revolved around veterans returning home and taking positions as team members or coaches. This was especially the case in the USA. It is less clear how amphetamine became so closely integrated into professional and amateur cycling, both in North America and in Europe. However, since cyclists had a history of stimulant use it is reasonable to assume any potential drug that became available would be experimented with and, if it worked, regularly put to use.

5   The steroids epidemic, 1945–1976

Introduction

Steroids have been the drugs most associated with doping since the late 1960s. They are responsible for remarkable improvements in performance. They have a visible effect on the shape of athletes' bodies, leading to what William Taylor called 'monstrous athletes' (1985). The craze for bodybuilding in the 1970s led to a number of high profile steroid users becoming famous for their physique and power. Some, such as Arnold Schwarzenegger, became international celebrities. The effect of steroids on women was very controversial, leading to accusations that women had denied their femininity in their efforts to succeed in sport. When steroid use spread to other sports and was clearly implicated in Olympic events, the landscape of sport, doping and anti-doping changed forever.

Steroids presented an entirely different set of problems from amphetamines. Steroids would be used much more widely by amateur and recreational athletes particularly in power sports such as bodybuilding. A huge black market developed after a range of new products became available in the 1970s. Meanwhile, the health risks were a lot more serious than those related to amphetamine use. Scientists warned that playing around with hormones would disrupt natural physiological functions and lead to a range of short-term side effects and potentially early deaths. However, when steroids first became available they were met with caution, not for their impact on health, but due to doubts over their effectiveness. So even though the first signs of usage came as early as the late 1940s, it was really the early 1960s that saw wider acceptance of their value for strength and fitness development. By then, the issue was political and needs to be understood in the context of the Cold War.

The science behind steroids

A small number of scientists had experimented with hormonal treatments from animals through the nineteenth and into the twentieth centuries. In 1848 a German scientist, Berthold, constructed an experiment in which he removed the testes of four roosters and implanted them in two capons (castrated roosters). He observed the capons for six months and reported that 'these animals remained male in regard to voice, reproduction instinct, fighting spirit, and growth of comb and wattle ... is maintained by the productive influence of the testicle' (cited in Taylor 1991: 5). This form of investigation was developed 50 years later by French scientist Charles-Édouard Brown-Séquard, who removed the testicles of dogs and guinea pigs which he brewed with a salt solution to create a 'testicle stew' which he injected into his own body. He was 72 years old at the time, and he addressed the Société de Biologie in Paris with claims that the 'stew' had increased his physical strength and his intellectual energy, as well as making the curious claim that it had lengthened the arc of his urine (Taylor 1991: 6; Hoberman 2005: 37).

Unfortunately this wonderful innovation did not benefit him long, he died soon after of unrelated causes. His legacy is a complex one. He did show an interest in the sorts of human hormone changes that would become much more popular and empirically valid in the twentieth century. John Hoberman claims he was the 'progenitor' of human replacement therapy or organotherapy and 'brought into being a hormone market that has greatly expanded over the past hundred years' (2005: 38). William Taylor is more circumspect, arguing that even though he established a series of notable advances in medical science especially in the field of human diseases, his reputation was besmirched by the testicle stew:

> he died one of the most discredited scientists in the history of medicine. The response of the scientific world was to break into laughter that can still be heard occasionally in some medical circles today. The very idea of testicular extracts affording such strength, endurance, and vitality! And for his perceived scientific blunder, Brown-Séquard had critics who have tried to wipe him completely off the scientific map.
>
> (1991: 6)

If he was treated harshly by his contemporaries, it was an unfair assessment of a lifetime devoted to science and to intellectual rigour. The scientific world may not have been ready for hormone replacement in the late nineteenth century, but that would change within a few decades and pharmaceutical companies saw the potential.

In 1926 Squibb Pharmaceuticals funded research at the University of Chicago by Professor Fred C. Koch and Lemuel C. McGee into the search for the male sex hormone. They drew testicular extract from bulls, injected it into capons and – after repeating the experiment to be sure – confirmed the capon had become more like a rooster: the sex hormone existed (McGee 1927; Taylor 1991). And so began the modern day quest to isolate, describe and synthesise the male sex hormone. A subsequent group of Chicago researchers headed by Koch experimented on a human eunuch with extract of bulls' testicles in a project funded by the National Research Council's Committee for Research in Problems of Sex (Taylor 1991: 7). The secretions from testes were shown to restore or enhance certain 'male' characteristics: the potential applications for society were exciting whether in the fields of public health, military power or competitive sport. As already discussed, it was hormones that most appealed to exercise physiologists such as Peter Karpovich and Ove Bøje.

This race for further discoveries became international and industry sponsors were desperate to profit from the patents. In 1934 a German scientist, Adolf Butenandt, managed to isolate 'small quantities of the androgenic hormone androsterone from 15,000 litres of urine sourced from Berlin's policemen' (Lenehan 2003: 64). Other researchers in the field included Kochakian who showed that testosterone affected the sexual characteristics of castrated dogs and male eunuchs (Lenehan 2003). On the verge of a breakthrough, the competition was divided according to funding and nationality:

> Research teams, sponsored by three rival chemical companies, tried to find more effective testosterone. Butenandt's group was funded by Schering. Another unit was backed by Organon from Holland. But it was Polish scientist Leopold Ruzicka, working for Ciba, who, in 1935, managed to beat the others and patented a process for the artificial preparation of testosterone.
>
> (Lenehan 2003: 64)

For their work in the field, Ruzicka and Butenandt were both awarded the 1939 Nobel Chemistry Prize but the latter declined due to the politics of the Second World War. By this stage, synthetic testosterone could be manufactured and further experiments were conducted by scientists interested in finding health-related applications for testosterone (Taylor 1991). CIBA, Schering and Roche-Organon were among the companies who had launched products based on the hormone by the early 1940s. Schering was based in the USA and Germany and by the 1930s was marketing a product called Progynon-B as the 'true female sex hormone'. Even by this stage there were signs of conflict between science and business. The advertising drew from work by the eminent endocrinologist E. A. Doisy, a future Nobel Prize winner, who was so angry at the misuse of his research by Schering that the *Journal of the American Medical Association* censured the company for its 'reprehensible' advertising campaign. These problems persisted as the company sold other hormone-based drugs in the 1940s (Hoberman 2005: 50). CIBA would be responsible for developing Dianabol for the sports market. So by the late 1940s the conditions were in place for steroids to impact upon sport: the basic research had proved promising, entrepreneurial companies showed an opportunity and, as shown by incidents from the previous few decades, athletes were prepared to experiment with whatever might help them.

Steroids in sport, 1945–1960

A number of writers have argued that steroids were manufactured and refined for physical performance purposes by the Nazi party during the Second World War. Houlihan offers the claim that steroids 'were used [in the 1940s] for the non-medical purpose of increasing the aggressiveness and strength of German soldiers' (1999: 45). Unfortunately, he fails to cite any supporting evidence. John Hoberman discusses in some detail the myth of Nazi steroid science (1992) but it remains impossible to judge with any real certainty whether this myth has any basis in fact. There is no evidence available to support the claim. Regardless of the actuality, the myth does serve to support the broader association of steroids with exploitative, totalitarian regimes such as the Nazis, the German Democratic Republic and the Union of Soviet Socialist Republics.

However, as noted above the development of hormonal therapy was gathering pace in the United States by the 1940s. In 1945 the American magazine *Business Week* proclaimed 'Of all the sex hormones, testosterone is said to have the greatest market potential' (cited in Hoberman 2005: 3). Also in that year, Paul de Kruif published the influential book, *The Male Hormone,* which outlined a highly positive appraisal of the drug's potential. He argued that it could enhance the sex drive of men and women, and that the established medical societies such as the AMA were not taking it seriously because of its connections with sexual activity. Despite this, doctors were recommending hormones for a range of ailments, notably those related to the ageing process. De Kruif used it himself, claiming that it extended his sense of vitality and manhood even though he was in his mid fifties.

The potential for athletes was not lost on de Kruif:

> We know both the St. Louis Cardinals and St. Louis Browns have won championships, super-charged by vitamins. It would be interesting to watch the productive power of an industry or a professional group that would try a systematic supercharge with testosterone – of course under a good hormone hunter's supervision.
>
> (de Kruif 1945, cited in Taylor 1991: 16)

The question of who first used steroids for sporting competition has yet to be conclusively answered. Anecdotal evidence, to be treated with some caution, suggests that bodybuilders in California indulged in the aftermath of de Kruif's book (Yesalis *et al.* 1993). This might make sense given other circumstantial details such as the first known scientific experiment linking steroids and sport. In 1944 a group of American researchers treated six men with methyltestosterone (supplied by Schering under the name Oreton-M) for 3–6 week periods to test their physical responses (Simonsen *et al.* 1944). The result was 'enhancement of central nervous system reflex time, back strength muscle enhancement, and increases in dynamic and static work performance' (Taylor 1991: 14). These conclusions were published in the *Journal of Clinical Endocrinology.* We cannot say for certain if research led to athletes' consumption, but the information was available at the time for those looking for enhancement products. And the experiment must have set out to test a hypothesis. In other words, the results might have firmed up speculations that had been circulating for some time.

However, the association of steroids with corrupt regimes fits neatly with the standard historical account of how these drugs were introduced to Western sport. This story begins in 1954 when a Soviet doctor at the World Weightlifting Championships in Vienna told his American counterpart, Dr John Zeigler, that his team had been enhanced by testosterone (Voy 1991). Zeigler, and other American sports doctors were allegedly unaware of the potential application of steroids in sport. The protagonists in this story supposedly make for reliable witnesses, mostly Zeigler himself who later in his career openly discussed his role in the development of steroids for American athletes. So it seems this is the first confirmed use of the drugs for competition. It is curious though that the Americans had not thought of using testosterone or steroids in sport before 1954. After all, it was in use and given the various claims made for hormonal treatment by drugs companies and researchers (Hoberman 2005), it seems very unlikely that Zeigler had to be told by a Soviet doctor that testosterone was useful for bodybuilding. In constructing this story, however, American writers such as Bob Goldman *et al.* (1984) and Robert Voy (1991) took Zeigler's account as fact and allowed him the opportunity to express not only regret at the ways in which the drug was abused, but also some positive self-appraisal as he claimed to have sought a safe way of allowing athletes to use steroids. It also led to Western writers uncritically accepting the idea that the USA were only reacting to Soviet behaviour:

> The 1950s, the era of the Cold War, saw the introduction of perhaps the most devastating drug known to Olympic sport. In the Soviet Union, in an effort to facilitate increases in the strength and power of their athletes, officials and medical personnel gave many of their athletes injections of testosterone. This appeared to give athletes who took it an advantage, and the Soviet Olympic medal tallies increased. To combat this unwelcome competition, some US athletes introduced a medical counter-measure, and began using steroids.
>
> (Toohey and Veal 2000: 143)

Similarly, Pat Lenehan argues that Zeigler only found out about Soviets using steroids in 1954 and that he then decided 'his own team needed to get even' (2003: 64). It seems most reasonable to assume groups in both the USA and the USSR were developing knowledge on steroids from the early 1950s onwards. John Zeigler's partnership with CIBA to produce Dianabol had coincided with a boom in bodybuilding cultures (Woodland 1980). The quest for more strength and muscle mass quickly led to problems. Zeigler told the journalist Bil Gilbert in 1969, 'The trouble was that the [users] went crazy about steroids. They figured if one pill was good, three or four would be better, and they were eating them like candy. I began seeing prostate trouble, and a couple of cases of atrophied testes' (Gilbert 1969: 70).

The myth of Nazi science, the accusation that Soviets 'started it', and Zeigler's later remorse, actually mask a more complex and intriguing story. Evidence from people who worked with Zeigler suggests that while he was a good community physician, he was also something of an eccentric and a man interested in pioneering experimentation. John Fair's (1993) account of the development of Dianabol in the context of wider scientific, political and sporting cultures of the time is a much underrated contribution to this history. Fair's interviews, including that with former Olympian, Mr America and Mr Universe, John Grimek, shed new light on the way in which the drug was tested and developed. Grimek worked with Zeigler and claimed he had developed a relationship with CIBA pharmaceutical company before 1954 who supplied him with testosterone for 'experimental purposes' (1993: 4). Just as importantly, it seems CIBA had somehow managed to provide the doctor with 'books and records from Germany where similar experiments were carried out by the Nazis' (1993: 4). This does suggest that the Nazis did work with steroids, a fact that could support that Nazis-as-inventors myth. However, not only was research being conducted in America around the same time, but Zeigler and CIBA were unethically using research data from potentially inhumane trials. Regardless of these issues, Zeigler, and presumably CIBA, wanted to know if the drugs would enhance the physique of already 'bulked up' bodybuilders and weightlifters.

In 1952, Zeigler worked with athletes who used the York gym in Pennsylvania. He persuaded the then Mr America, Jim Park, featherweight champion Yas Kuzuhara and John Grimek to try the testosterone. Although this raft of tests proved unsuccessful – the athletes failed to see the impacts of the drugs and felt 'lousy' – Grimek was still trying out Zeigler's 'chemical substances' in 1954 (Fair 1993: 4–5). This was two years after Bob Hoffman accused Soviet weightlifters of using hormones in the 1952 Olympics. When the USA team went to the world championships in Vienna in October 1954, the Soviets accused them of stimulating the athletes with some kind of drug. And yet, it was precisely at this event that Zeigler later claimed he was informed by a Soviet doctor 'after a few drinks' that some of his team were using testosterone (Fair 1993: 4). While Zeigler must have been frustrated with the 1952 failures, he was also angry at the Soviets' accusations, and probably irritated that the Soviets seemed to have found a way of successfully applying testosterone. Due to other work commitments, he did not return to this puzzle until the late 1950s.

By this stage, the politics of the Cold War had taken a radical turn, and sport was increasingly being dragged in to the propaganda and vitriol. The Soviet Union did not initially enter the Olympic Movement after the Second World War partly because of a certain disaffection between the IOC and the Soviet government. The former had been irritated by Russia's role in helping organise Worker Games in 1932 and 1936 parallel to the Olympic Games. As a result, the President of the IOC from 1952–1972, Avery Brundage, was ambivalent about the USSR joining the first post-war Games in London (Riordan 1993: 28). For their part, the Soviet Government condemned the IOC after an article published ahead of the 1948 Games in a Soviet magazine claimed that the

> Olympics were run by capitalists and aristocrats, that workers had little chance of competing, that racial discrimination against Jews and Blacks had occurred in Berlin in 1936 and would be applied against East Europeans who, in any case, might well be corrupted and recruited as spies.
>
> (cited in Riordan 1993: 27)

On top of which Stalin had been strongly opposed to Soviet participation in the Olympics. The dialogue among IOC members highlighted their fundamental suspicion of communist societies just as the USSR's military power, development of nuclear technology, and expansion into Eastern Europe, proved to be catalysts for the intense political and ideological rivalry known as the Cold War. An IOC Executive Committee Member, Colonel P. W. Scharoo, reported in November 1947 that the highly organised system for sport in the USSR was being used for nationalist purposes by the government. His derisive comments reflected an emerging popular stereotype, 'In Russia nobody is free and independent. Individuals are only numbers in the state' (cited in Riordan 1993: 28). Indeed, the discursive construction of a polarised world of opposing cultures and politics was reinforced in March of that same year in the American President Harry Truman's speech to Congress on the threat of communism that included the following:

> At the present moment in world history nearly every nation must choose between alternative ways of life. The choice is too often not a free one. One way of life is based upon the will of the majority ... The second is based upon the will of a minority forcibly imposed upon the majority. It relies upon terror and oppression, a controlled press and radio, fixed elections and the suppression of personal freedoms.
>
> (Truman 1955, cited in Saunders 1999: 25)

Brundage fell in line with this, 'According to Communist philosophy, every person and everything is subservient to the State' (cited in Riordan 1993: 29). He remained suspicious of Soviet 'shamateurism', the puritanical and regimented nature of their sports, and the explicit connection made between sport and national prestige (Hoberman 1992: 194). Nonetheless, the IOC could not deny the USSR entry because such a decision would contradict their determination to keep politics out of sport. The u-turn among the Soviets was prompted by a number of factors, including the opportunity to assert the success of their political ideology on the most salient of all international stages. In return for his acquiescence, however, Stalin was sent a 'special note' to 'guarantee victory' by the Chairman of the government Committee on Physical Culture and Sport, Nikolai Romanov (Riordan 1993: 26). The full weight of the Soviet hierarchy was behind sport now, and that meant a systematic application of doping medicine and science to the problem of achieving excellence and, more pertinently, gaining supremacy over the USA and its allies.

Given this, it is understandable that the bodybuilder Samuel Fussell attributed Zeigler's development of steroids to the 'interest of national prestige' (cited in Fair 1993: 2). There is no doubt American sports physicians from the 1950s through to the late 1970s (at least) made the connection between politics and doping: defeat in athletic competition to the communists had to be avoided at all costs, drugs were seen as protecting American values and freedoms (Goldman *et al.* 1984). However, even when Zeigler approached weightlifters in 1959 for further experimentation, the athletes were wary it would disrupt their training for the 1960 Olympic Games. Bob Hoffman, then coach to the American squad and editor of

Strength and Health magazine, was initially reluctant to take part because he failed to see the potential of Zeigler's testosterone. But he returned from the European Championships in May 1960 with more suspicions about Soviet use of drugs. By the mid 1960s, John Grimek was again trying testosterone and had helped recruit weightlifters, Bill March and Tony Garcy, to take part in further experiments. The results were inconclusive but Hoffman had been persuaded to give a select few of the Olympic lifters doses of steroids during the 1960 Games 'with no knowledge of appropriate timing of doses' (Fair 1993: 7). The results were unclear, and even after the Games athletes remained sceptical of the power of these little pills to produce significant improvements in performance (Fair 1993).

Spread of steroids, 1960–1968

The spread of steroids into other sports seems to have happened in the first years of the 1960s by which time there were types on the market. Users could turn to various testosterone derivates including Halotestin (fluoxymesterone), Adroyd (oxymetholone), Durabolin (nandrolone phenpropionate) and stanozolol (Winstrol) (Fruehan and Frawley, 1963; Lenehan 2003: 65). Bob Hoffman knew by then what the drugs could do, having experimented with them himself for six weeks in the aftermath of the 1960 Rome Games. He admitted that steroids had 'increased my strength. In five days I could curl and press more and I gained weight' (cited in Fair 1993: 9). Although he did not admit this at the time, he clearly had more confidence in the effectiveness of steroids. It would take until 1967 before he went public with this information in his own *Strength and Health* magazine (Hoffman 1967). In between times, Zeigler continued to develop a range of strategies for strength training, mixing the new technique of isometrics, with steroids and the mental training technique of hypnosis. While the steroids were kept secret, the isometrics were publicised through Hoffman's magazine and he sold a range of products designed to help aspiring bodybuilders emulate the achievements of champions whose diet, in some cases, was also boosted by drugs though that part was kept a secret (Fair 1993).

By 1962, Zeigler was working with Winthrop Pharmaceuticals to find a better form of steroid. He developed a close relationship with Louis Riecke from New Orleans, who had won the Junior Nationals in 1955. Between 1960 and 1962, Zeigler helped Riecke with innovative methods and with drugs. After various highs and lows, they developed a more effective steroid programme by 1962 which consisted of four tablets a day, but realised they take about four weeks to have much impact. Knowledge was improving and Reicke reported positive results from the Winthrop pills and from Dianabol in conjunction with isometric exercises and mental attitude training (Fair 1993: 20). Under Zeigler's guidance, he tied for first at the 1963 Senior Nationals, broke the world snatch record in 1964 and while he made the Olympic team he was injured during the event and retired from competition. His colleague, Bill March, a fellow Zeigler protégé, won five world championships between 1961 and 1965, set a world record for press-ups, and achieved top five places in international competitions (Fair 1993). It had taken some persuasion, the force of Zeigler's personality and conviction, some difficult experiments, and a combination programme, to prove that steroids did work. Although the drugs were kept from public view, there is no doubt this period proved a watershed for demonstrating that they ought to be part of any serious competitor's training strategy. It seems unlikely that the Soviets were first in this particular race, and Zeigler's later remorse sits uneasily with his claims in 1965 that his overall aim was to achieve 'physical performances now considered SUPERHU-MAN!' (cited in Fair 1993: 23). The years between the 1960 Rome Olympics and the 1964 Tokyo Games were pivotal for American (and probably other Western countries') use of steroids. The experimentation had proved invaluable, and drug companies battled it out to find the best products. Zeigler's legacy was not just the first applications of testosterone, but in proving to a sceptical world of weight trainers and their coaches that steroids were the way forward.

The consequences were clear by the 1964 Olympic Games. The American shot-putter who took gold at the 1956 Games, Harold Connolly started using them in 1964 and continued through to 1972 (*New York Times*, 14 July 1973). Vials were again found in a speed skater's changing room at the Winter Games in 1964 (Prokop 1975). And a survey of British Olympic athletes showed 15 per cent had taken some form of drug as part of their preparation for the 1964 Games (Williams 1974: 130). A later admission of steroid use came from Americans Dallas Long and Randy Matson in that event (*New York Times*, 17 October 1971; Gilbert 1969).

Personal testimony from 1964 showed that steroids were being used by the Americans as much as by the Soviets. Some British coaches were surprised and dismayed by what they discovered at the Games. This report was made by Tom McNab, international level athletes coach in the 1960s and 1970s:

> in the 1964 Olympics I was there as an observer with my old friend, the late Ron Pickering, and Ron came back with me one day to the hotel at which we were staying, telling me that the American team were taking various pills at breakfast time, vitamins and some new thing called anabolic steroids which they were taking at breakfast. But I'd never heard of such things and it meant very little to me but progressively over the next six years it became clear that body-building drugs were being taken, as there were some pretty substantial changes in performance, particularly in the throws and decathlon.
> (McNab 1993: 48)

Within two years the drug had spread among other Western athletes. The British discus thrower Bill Tancred, said that he 'first heard about them at the 1966 Commonwealth Games from competitors from other countries' (*The Times*, 1 November 1973). However, Tancred's efforts to assuage British guilt were not supported by others. The physical educationalist from Birmingham University, A. H. Payne, claimed that steroids were being used by British athletes 'more and more' by 1966 and that 'several' had used them for the Commonwealth Games in Jamaica that year (1975: 83).

It was not just Olympic and Commonwealth Games sports that faced the growing problem of steroid use. It spread through the ranks of American sport through the next few years:

> It is an assumption, based on reasonably good but unverifiable reports, that some players on almost every NFL and AFL team have used anabolic steroids. It is a fact, according to physicians, that, in addition to the San Diego Chargers, members of the Kansas City Chiefs, Atlanta Falcons and Cleveland Browns have taken the drug. Ken Ferguson of Utah State University, who went on to play professional football in Canada, has said that 90% of college linemen have used steroids. 'I'd say anybody who has graduated from college to professional football in the last four years has used them', said Ferguson in 1968. So widespread is the faith in hormones that there are verified incidents where pro scouts have supplied the drug to college draftees, and college recruiters have given it to high school players.
>
> (Gilbert 1969: 70–71)

The hammer throwing competition is a good example to draw upon to show how steroids impacted upon elite sports performance. The world record holder between 1956 and 1965 was the American Harold Connolly who would admit to a US Congress Inquiry in 1973 that he had been 'hooked' on steroids between 1964 and 1972. His first world record had been set at 68.54 metres in 1956. His last and steroid-assisted world record was in 1965 at 71.26 metres. His career declined after that despite the drugs. It is probable that the world records set over the next 10 years were assisted by steroids, given there was no testing carried out either in or out of competition events and a self-confessed user at the top level could not keep up with the record breaking. The record was regularly broken by throwers from the Soviet Union, Hungary and West Germany. By 1975, the year before steroid testing was introduced to the Olympics, the record was held by German Walter Schmidt at 79.30 metres. In other words, the record was improved upon by less than 3 metres in the nine years between 1956 and 1965, and then by almost 8 metres in the ten years between 1965 and 1975.[1]

As a final reflection on this period, it does seem that taking steroids did no harm to Connolly's long-term reputation: as if he had not done that much wrong. He was inducted into the National Throw Coaches Association Hall of Fame in November 2005. The following month, his alma mater Boston College unveiled a memorial statue in his honour (Oslin 2006). The publicity surrounding both occasions failed to mention doping, as if this has to be airbrushed from his personal history and from American sports history. But why should Connolly be exonerated when so many others, like the Soviets of his day or Ben Johnson later, continue to be demonised? Perhaps the reason lies with the commonly held theory that Americans who used steroids were only doing it as part of the good fight against communism.

The growing phenomenon, 1968–1976

Given the impact the drugs were obviously having, it is no surprise that steroid use increased rapidly in the late 1960s. The British international shot-putter, Jeff Teale, used them between 1967 and 1972 during which time he won a silver medal at the Commonwealth Games and the Amateur Athletics Association championship twice (Woodland 1980: 56–7).

The 1968 Olympics were affected by steroids. Professor Arnold Beckett said 'Let's face it – these will be used in Mexico' (*The Times*, 10 September 1968). Further confirmation came from Tom Wandell, a physician and decathlete at those Games. He claimed that during the pre-Games high altitude training camp more than a third of the American track and field team were using steroids (*New York Times*, 17 October 1971). Payne claimed that:

> In the 1968 Olympics, I am sure that one of the factors involved in the magnificent performances was that the use of steroids had by then become widespread. It was rumoured that athletes in all events up to and including the 1500 metres in the American team were given steroids by their coaches.
>
> (1975: 83)

There was of course no test for steroids at this time, and there appears to have been little ethical debate among athletes about how best to make the most of this new chemical technology.

The media were beginning to take such an interest to report on users who would make public admissions. For instance, in 1970 *The Times* reported that the world record shot-putter, American Randy Matson took them but stopped when they were banned by the IOC. Other athletes were encouraged to join in this reportage. The Italian triple jumper Giuseppe Gentile told Neil Allen of *The Times* that 'on a recent stay in California he found a large number of American athletes taking steroids' (*The Times*, 15 April 1970). At the same time, Arthur Gold, then Secretary of the British Amateur Athletic Association, suggested that drug taking was 'one of sport's chief problems' and that 'shot-putting should be excluded from international athletics until a fool-proof method of detecting the taking of anabolic steroids was discovered' (*The Times*, 15 April 1970).

By the early 1970s it became obvious that steroids were on the increase and spreading from power sports to explosive events such as sprinting, hurdling and rugby. Dr Donald Cooper, Director of Health Services at Oklahoma State University and the United States team physician at the 1968 Games said, 'We know that drugs are being used by athletes more than anyone officially has knowledge of' (*New York Times*, 24 January 1971). The American Government and public were finding out what happened behind the scenes in professional sport:

> In testimony before a California legislative subcommittee inquiring into drug abuse in sport, Paul Lowe, a former all-pro running back for the San

Diego Chargers, claimed pink steroid pills were placed next to each player's plate on the dining table in the Charger training camp. According to Lowe, there was a clear implication that players who refused to take the pills would be fined. Additionally, Lowe and other Charger players claim they were not even informed in advance that the pills were steroids.

(Scott 1971)

In some cases, athletes argued in favour of steroid use. Some imagined they were necessary 'to compete on level terms with the rest of the world at the Munich Olympic Games' (*The Times*, 21 April 1972). The British Olympic show jumper Harvey Smith provoked controversy when he wrote in his book *V for Victory* that drugs should be allowed, otherwise 'our athletes are like drivers of a racing car with one gear less than their rivals' (*The Times*, 27 November 1972). Smith's comments may not have encouraged others to be more open about doping, but they do suggest that drugs were used at this time by athletes.

Writing in the *Guardian*, John Williams argued that:

For some years now it has been known that certain athletes in the power events have taken these body building drugs in enormous doses in combination with very heavy weight training programmes and high protein diets. The results are in the records books for all to see.

(23 August 1972)[2]

He was aware of the uncertainties around efficacy and side effects that had held back some users. As a result, he was concerned that 'controlled clinical trials ... indicate that these drugs are effective for the sportsman's purpose', and that 'it now seems very likely that in lower doses anabolic steroids are, at least in the short run, safe'. Later in the same year, the British Association of National Coaches conference brought steroid use to the attention of the Sports Council, then chaired by Dr Roger Bannister. Speaking at the conference, the British Olympic weightlifting coach, John Lear, offered a startling portrayal of the situation:

How does one deal with a sport in which cheating is so prevalent that it is no longer considered cheating? My future role as a coach at international level has already been described as that of a 'needle' man. It is a role I will continue to reject.

(*The Times*, 14 October 1972)

The British national athletics coach, Wilf Paish, said in a 1972 BBC Panaroma documentary that athletes in track and field needed steroids to have a chance of winning and that he would direct young athletes to a doctor to get the pills. Paish said:

I'm in an awkward situation but I don't condemn them at all. It's difficult for me to condone them in my position but I certainly don't condemn them.

Because I feel athletics is wanting to be the best, the best in the world. And it's very difficult to be the best in the world these days unless you're on steroids because I'm fairly certain the standards set throughout the world are influenced by athletes who have or still do take this drug ... I feel now it's got so far that we can't beat them we're almost going to have to join them.

(cited in BBC 2005a)

Steroids were widely used in the 1972 Olympics. An unofficial poll of competitors was conducted by the then world discus record holder Jay Silvester. Respondents came from the USA, USSR, Egypt, New Zealand, Canada, Morocco and Britain. He found that two-thirds had previously used steroids, the vast majority had used them within the six months leading up to the Games (Woodland 1980: 57). In the aftermath, Silvester spoke to the British press. He said, 'All the throwers and weightlifters and "heavies" of any ability in these Olympics have taken or do take the illegal anabolic steroids' (*The Times*, 24 August 1972). He claimed this was a necessary part of sport, 'if you don't take steroids you are bound to be handicapped in the heavy events. So guys who really want to do well have to take a calculated risk' (*The Times*, 24 August 1972). Silvester made a number of interesting observations about how doping worked in different countries. While Western athletes were allowed to make 'their own decision' he feared that the medical support was better in the Eastern bloc, 'one hopes that, like in the communist countries, they get proper medical advice' (*The Times*, 24 August 1972). In another veiled criticism of the American establishment's failings compared to Britain, he said, 'At least you've got people admitting it gives you strength whereas some of our doctors here, good men in many ways, try to kid us that the pills have no real effect' (*The Times*, 24 August 1972). However, Ludwig Prokop was much more scathing about the cynical role sports doctors were playing at this time, 'right up to the latest period [i.e. the Olympic Games in Munich], again and again many doping substances will be introduced via the opportunity of some medical treatment declared to be absolutely necessary' (1975: 86).

By 1974 some athletes were becoming tired and cynical about the steroids epidemic. The Olympic pentathlon gold medallist, Mary Peters, wrote in her autobiography:

Not long ago a medical research team in the United States attempted to set up extensive research into the effects of steroids on weightlifters and throwers, only to discover that there were so few who *weren't* taking them that they couldn't establish any worthwhile comparisons.

(cited in Woodland 1980: 57)

By this stage, the capitalist versus communist divide had created a double-bind situation. Both sides suspected each other of using steroids, and neither was going to back down. British track and field athletes in the early 1970s accused East Europeans of being on steroids and complained that 'in those countries the taking of drugs by athletes is a highly organised affair in which doctors are involved and in which regular monitoring of the athletes' condition is carried out' (Payne 1975: 87). The American view of the USSR was, as John Zeigler put it, that 'an individual is worth absolutely nothing' (1984: 1). The American bodybuilder Bob Goldman highlighted the political motivations of sports doctors who gave athletes steroids:

> Certainly, patriotism was a factor. Getting beaten on the playing fields, as well as in outer space and the Cold War, was a hard-to-swallow pill for American doctors who had been raised on American virtue-will-out based supremacy. The feeling of these doctors was that if they could in any way help an American athlete bring home the gold, they had somehow struck a blow for freedom. Moreover, these doctors were convinced that all of the Eastern European athletes were gulping Sputnik-era growth-and-strength steroids, thus gaining an unfair advantage over Western competitors. To the doctor who equated victory on the athletic field with a victory in the political arena, the choice seemed to be to give drugs or risk an American humiliation and open the door to Communism.
>
> (1984: 73)

These doctors fed a popular habit. The American medical expert on steroids, Dr James Wright wrote in 1978, 'As of 1977, based on personal observations and interviews with numerous athletes in the strength related sports, I would estimate that over 90% use steroids on a regular basis' (cited in Taylor 1991: 28). Later evidence would show that the USSR and GDR had a large-scale system for doping athletes. It seems that both sides were culpable even if both had their own self-justifications.

It is clear that steroid usage grew quickly after the early experiments of the 1950s and 1960s. There was a race between 'East' and 'West' to find the best applications and increase medal hauls. Documents recovered from sports science labs in the GDR by former athletes who defected to the West, Brigitte Berendonk and Franke Werner, showed that the steroid Oral-Turinabol had been given in regular and large doses to GDR Olympians under the government scheme State Plan 14.25 (Ungerledier 2001). The GDR and USSR histories of doping have become the most notorious and most widely criticised. Perhaps that is because the athletes were not always informed of the drugs they were being given, or because of the court cases of the early twenty-first century in which athletes sued the German state for compensation to cover the health consequences of doping. Also, the role of the state is seen as highly problematic: Western traditions have it that the state should protect citizens and set a proper moral standard. However, evidence from the West suggests that the usual stereotypes and blaming only tell part of the story (Dimeo 2006). The Zeigler and Hoffman partnership helped develop steroids in America, and from there they spread throughout Western sport. However, the wider scientific community struggled to put together a coherent response to steroids.

The science of performance effects and health

By the late 1960s and into the 1970s a few scientists were taking an interest in steroids. One of the key questions was whether or not they were effective and how safe they were to use. An editorial in the *British Medical Journal* stated that 'Anabolic steroid combined with high protein diet might have an anticatabolic effect under conditions of severe muscular exercise and hence produce an increase in physical performance' (1967: 310). Such public pronouncements could only lead to increased patterns of usage among athletes, especially if the health warnings were either muted or entirely ignored.

Elsewhere, studies began to ask if steroids were having the effects athletes claimed and desired. L. C. Johnson and J. P. O'Shea of Oregon State University conducted a study using methandrostenolone (Dianabol) combined with a high protein supplement on weightlifters over a three-week period (1969). The basis for the study was that steroids were 'increasingly widespread' and 'many instances of extraordinary and rapid improvement have been reported'. However, they acknowledged that these were anecdotal cases and that rumoured side effects also needed to be investigated. Their findings, published in *Science*, showed that strength, muscle mass, oxygen uptake ability and nitrogen retention by the blood, were also increased. They found no problematic physiological side effects.

A year later, O'Shea conducted a study of the same drug on competitive swimmers. He found that, 'as an ergogenic aid anabolic steroid treatment alone is ineffective in improving athletic performance' (1970: 342). However, he did suggest that the combination of steroids and protein may have different results. A further study at Oregon used weightlifters and swimmers as subjects to test the effects of oxandrolone (Anavar) over an 11-week period. O'Shea and Winkler concluded that, 'No toxic side effects such as edema, impaired hepatic function, or changes in electrolyte balance were noted. Strength performance was significantly increased in weightlifters. There was no evidence that steroid treatment had any effect on improving performance (speed) in competitive swimmers' (1970: 351).

Using the more advanced double-blind method, meaning that a control group is given a placebo to counteract the possibility that the steroids act as a placebo, O'Shea tested 20 weightlifters over a four-week period with methandrostenolone. He found that with the protein supplement there were 'significant increases in dynamic strength' and 'no evidence of androgenic symtomology' (1971: 363). This contradicted other studies such as that by Fowler *et al.* (1965) which showed steroids to have no effect on strength. Indeed, about half of the 20 studies conducted between 1965 and 1976 showed an effect and the other half showed no effect (Taylor 1991).

The central factor in explaining this discrepancy was recognised in 1982 by William Taylor, a weight training medical doctor from the United States who would campaign for two decades against steroids in sport. His starting point was to show that the anecdotal evidence from users was indeed correct: steroids did improve performance. To do so, he demonstrated that those studies which found no effect had used subjects that had been previously trained using weights resistance methods:

> the studies involving the untrained subjects were not able to delineate the gains in muscle mass and strength from *learning* to lift weights and the effects of anabolic steroids ... the athletic subjects were unable to benefit from anabolic steroid use over and above the training effect of the study design itself. On the other hand, if the athletic subject was already weight-trained and then the anabolic steroids were used, the effects of the steroids were seen. The studies with previously weight-trained subjects showed that anabolic steroids enhanced muscle mass and strength over and above the effects of weight training alone.
>
> (1991: 31)

Further confirmation of Taylor's finding was made after statistical analysis of the literature in the field by Haupt and Rovere (1984). This marked a distinctive shift from the official version of science in this field. Up until the mid 1970s the range of studies had seemed to contradict each other, so the major sports medicine bodies in America and Britain set out to establish a definitive statement. In 1975 the BASM, with Lord Porritt now the President, organised a conference in London called 'Anabolic Steroids in Sport' and brought together delegates from around the world. A study presented by D. L. J. Freed and A. J. Banks (1975) of Manchester University used the double-blind, placebo controlled method and experienced weight-trained athletes. This showed that moderate doses over six weeks did improve performance. However, according to Taylor (1991) greater weight was given to a study by Professor G. R. Hervey of Leeds University which showed large doses to have had no effect on muscle mass and strength (1975). It was only years later though that the real reason for this was discovered. The graduate assistant working with Professor Hervey stole the drugs and sold them to users in a local gym. Years later, his college education proved to be of mixed benefit when he was convicted and imprisoned for steroid trafficking in the United States (Taylor 1991: 25).

Taylor argued that the BASM repeated for steroids what they had asserted for amphetamines that 'the only effective and safe way of ensuring optimum performance in any activity is a proper programme of training and preparation ... No known chemical agent is capable of producing both safely and effectively an improvement in performance in a healthy human subject'. It is the case that the BASM reprinted this with the claim that it 'continues to apply' (Editorial 1975a: 58). However, Taylor does overstate his case with respect to criticising the BASM. One of the stated conclusions of the symposium was, 'The actions of anabolic steroids in healthy, training athletes are not fully understood. Studies show conflicting results in respect of increase in body size, measures of strength and improvement in performance. The use of anabolics appears, however, to be widespread, in certain sports'. And since part of the symposium discussed new methods for testing (see Chapter 7), 'Detection methods for anabolic steroids, as well as naturally occurring hormones, are effective and we seek the wider spread of approved testing laboratories to eliminate the use of drugs in sport' (BASM, 1975b: 110). So the BASM did not take Hervey's flawed research as the definitive statement, as Taylor implies. Instead, they offer a balanced approach regarding the various studies conducted up to this point.

More convincing is the argument that the ACSM members denied the value of steroids for performance. Allan J. Ryan was a founding member of ACSM, President in 1963–4, and the creator and editor of the journal *The Physician and Sportsmedicine*. He regularly described steroids as 'fool's gold', claimed that their function as performance enhancers was a 'myth' and that any improvement was due to a placebo effect (Taylor 1991: 26). Ryan was supported by such public sports medics as Dan Hanley who at the time was a medical officer for the National Collegiate Athletic Association. At the 1976 annual meeting a very heated debate ensued involving the deniers against those whose research showed steroids did enhance performance, including L. C. Johnson of Oregon University and James Wright, author of *Anabolic Steroids and Sports* (1978). What convinced Johnson as much as the study he had helped conduct was that he had also been a subject: he had 'felt the powers of anabolic steroids on his own athletic performance' (Taylor 1991: 27). The ACSM concluded that the evidence was inconclusive. Education was the only way forward since experimental research was deemed unethical (though the ACSM did not emphasise testing as much as the BASM had). This prompted William Taylor's disgust:

> let's go educate: Anabolic steroids are placebos, and there are potential side effects from using them, but don't ask about the side effects because we really don't know what they are. Furthermore, we are going to make it unethical to study these effects in the doses that athletes are taking. That just about does it. The anabolic steroid problem now should just go away!
>
> (1991: 28)

The knowledge base on health is especially curious. In 1972 *The Times* quoted from an IOC booklet called *Doping* in which it was claimed that steroids 'can severely harm the health, causing liver and bone damage, disturbances in the metabolic and sexual functions, and, among women, virilization and menstrual upset' (*The Times*, 21 April 1972). Such fears were also expressed by George Kaye, physiology editor of the American magazine *Muscle Power* who is quoted as saying 'How nutsy must one be to risk liver damage, testes atrophy, prostate and kidney cancer?' By contrast, the more rational scientific opinion was offered by Professor F. T. G. Prutny who was researching detection methods at St Thomas' Hospital, London, and funded by the Sports Council. He argued there was a lack of evidence, but risks of vascular disease and cancer were possible though liver cell changes would be reversible after discontinuation of the drugs.

In fact, the biggest fears around this time period were about the masculinizing effects on women. Prutny claimed that he was certain steroids led to 'interference with the menstrual cycle, temporal recession of the hair and hypertrophy of the clitoris' (*The Times*, 21 April 1972). It is difficult to know the basis of such claims and how they might be measured in practice.

In sum, the scientific view of steroids was a delayed reaction thanks to confused research and hypothetical posturing. Perhaps it is unsurprising, as Chapter 7 shows, that a test for steroid use in sport was not established until 1975. Scientists were too busy arguing about strength effects and health issues to bother with the technical aspects of testing.

Conclusion

The historiography of steroids is somewhat confusing. The identification of the German Nazi Government in the 1930s and 1940s and the USSR in the 1950s as the pioneers of doping fits all too easily with other historical simplifications. People in the West do not want to imagine that Americans and Europeans deliberately set out to cheat in sports. It is easier and cosier to place steroids in the context of exploitative, inhumane, totalitarian regimes. The explanation for why 'our boys' felt compelled to take steroids lies almost in a militaristic sense of doing their duty for their country.

And yet the picture is actually much more complex. The story of Zeigler's experiments and connections with Hoffman and the bodybuilders shows a great deal of enthusiasm and energy went into doping with steroids. It was not a reluctant endeavour brought on by feelings of inferiority. It was, in Zeigler's words, an attempt to create superhuman performances. The response from the scientific community was slow and ambivalent. Studies initially seemed to show that steroids could only have a placebo effect. However, better studies soon contradicted such findings and despite some reluctance it was eventually accepted that steroids could improve strength performance. By this stage, the epidemic had set in and usage was internationally widespread. The scientific view of the health risks was also ambivalent. No study proved what many suspected.

Steroids literally changed sports by improving and strengthening the body. They reshaped bodies and increased their possibilities. They caused much more of a public issue than amphetamines ever had. Indeed, as the next two chapters will show, the authorities were largely unperturbed by amphetamine use. It was steroids that made scientists and sports authorities really wake up to the doping 'crisis'.

6   Dealing with the scandal

Anti-doping and the new ethics of sport, 1945–1965

Introduction

There is no doubt that sports doping took off during the years from 1945 through to the late 1960s. The structural reasons are obvious: availability of stimulant drugs; research and experience showing their effectiveness; expansion of the importance of sport in terms of national prestige and individual glory; the increasing use of sports science to enhance performance. What is less obvious is why various scientists, sports administrators, governments and journalists began to question the use of certain drugs by athletes. As shown in previous chapters, the idea that doping was wrong did not feature too strongly in the late nineteenth and first half of the twentieth century. So there is no ahistorical sense in which doping transgresses the values of sport. Instead, the origins of anti-doping are to be found in a specific time period, more specifically in the workings of a small group of scientists and administrators who managed to impose their view of ethics on to sport. The imagined universality of anti-doping ethics has been historically and culturally contingent: the product of networks of campaigners and broader social, political, and cultural circumstances that informed and framed the new ethics of sport.

The 1950s were an ambivalent period in doping history. John Hoberman uses a few examples of coaches who employed various physiological and psychological techniques to suggest that doping was seen as acceptable. Certainly, the evidence from Chapter 4 shows that some drugs were commonly used. In wider society, amphetamines were publicly available and sanctioned by government and commercial manufacturers. So even those who were using them were unlikely to see the problem, especially as there was no coherent anti-doping moralising, no testing, and no laws against drug use in sport. However, Hoberman overstates the case when he argues that during the 1950s doping was not considered to be a 'sin'. Several strong condemnations of drug use were made in public by interested medics, and by 1957 the AMA had begun taking the issue seriously.

It would be the very public tragedies involving Knud Enemark Jensen in 1960 and Tommy Simpson in 1967 that – despite their true complexities – were taken as simple moral tales that over-indulgence needed to be stopped. These occurred around the same time that wider social questions were being asked about drugs, either for medical or recreational purposes. The safety of medical drugs was challenged after the thalidomide scandal of 1961 when a drug given to pregnant women to treat morning sickness left their new born children with various physical deformities. The recreational excesses of anti-establishment or violent youth groups were increasingly associated with their indulgence in – among other drugs – amphetamines, heroin, cocaine and cannabis. Alcohol was the focus of a number of campaigns such as the ban on drinking and driving. In short, the paradigm of the 1940s in which drugs offered opportunities in sport and society, gave way to a new paradigm in which drugs were something to be feared and regulated. It was also informed by the wider critique of science in light of Nazi experiments in POW camps, eugenics, and nuclear technology. This change began slowly in the 1950s but underwent a radical reinforcement in the 1960s. The importance of this turnaround can hardly be overstated. It set the foundation for four decades of anti-doping struggle and the increasing criminalisation of drug use in sport; for the idealistic vision of drug-free sport that has consistently failed to materialise. It set in place the modernisation of anti-doping: a system that rigidly enforced moral values through scientific testing, legal restrictions, and bureaucratic procedures. It combined an international response to the problem, led initially by the CoE but reinforced by the IOC, with a new discourse in which drug taking was routinely described as an 'evil'. A strong rhetorical stance laid the foundation for stringent laws and procedures. Anti-doping got serious in the early 1960s: its emergence and consolidation needs to be more fully understood as it set the framework and rationale within which anti-doping policy and debate continue to operate.

Before doping was a sin?

In the mid 1950s, many coaches and doctors failed to see why drug use might be wrong. John Hoberman discusses the Australian swimming coach Forbes Carlile's accommodating attitude to the use of aspirin, potassium biphosphate and hypnosis, 'The crucial factor was the guilt-free mentality of those who were trying to reach and exceed human limits ... It simply did not occur to him that the use of performance aids might be unethical' (2005: 186). And in a broader reflection on the ethical issues in the 1950s, he argues, 'What counts is the mind-set of entitlement: athletes and their handlers feel that they are allowed to push back the limits of human performance however they can, since there are no ethical norms to say they should not' (2005: 186–7).

To make a similar point, Ivan Waddington refers to the frank discussion of Leslie Knighton's 'pep pill' episode in a book called *Forward, Arsenal* written by Bernard Joy in 1952. Joy presents the story in a straightforward factual way, without judgement or any suggestion that Knighton had been cheating: he 'saw nothing reprehensible in Arsenal's use of stimulants' (Waddington 2000: 99). What makes this more interesting is that Joy's own career was marked by a commitment to amateurism, having football to the highest level without turning professional. He was the last amateur to play for England, in 1936. Although drugs were common in the more professional sports such as cycling, and later became associated with the obsessive career orientation of professional athletes, the 1950s were a time when some amateurs saw little problem with turning to 'artificial' enhancements. Even Roger Bannister openly discussed the potential of extra oxygen (*Bulletin du Comité International Olympique*, 1954).

In 1958, the Olympic team doctor, sports medic and founder of BASM, Adolphe Abrahams set out a balanced discussion of doping. He claimed that if stimulants were available to all athletes there was no strong argument against using them:

> Suppose there are drugs that possess a stimulating or inhibiting action whereby athletic performance is enhanced whilst it is certain that no temporary or ultimate harm is in consequence incurred. These it must be submitted are free from secrecy, they must be universally available. What objection would be raised to their employment? Perhaps an uncomfortable feeling that – to use a familiar question-begging term – it would be unsporting to employ an advantage that the giants of the past did not enjoy.
>
> (Abrahams 1958: 27)

This was an important and influential doctor who had a close involvement with sport over several decades making public statements on the potential legitimacy of drugs in sport. Quite how representative Abrahams was of wider opinion is a matter of conjecture. Hoberman has claimed, in typical overstatement, that he opened 'the door to the legitimate use of performance-enhancing drugs by athletes' (2005: 185).

As much as Abrahams' opinions are interesting and probably were taken seriously by a number of people (they were first presented to the Society for the Study of Addiction), Hoberman's assessment cannot be fully accepted. Abrahams himself had fully qualified his statements on the basis of health, openness, access and even then was circumspect about the whole issue. If the doors to drug use had been opened, why was there such an angry reaction to Herbert Berger's accusation that the four-minute milers had used stimulants to help them? In fact, why did Berger even raise the issue in the first place. The most that can be said for the 1950s is that there was a divergence of opinion. While some individuals such as Carlile, Joy and Abrahams were taking the issue on balance, other anti-doping experts were beginning to establish the early groundwork for a more powerful movement.

The beginnings of anti-doping policy and science

The rising profile of doping as a health issue can be found even before Abrahams and the AMA's public discussions. Five years earlier, in February 1952 delegates at a major international conference in Oslo on the subject of health and sports heard health policy experts address the question. The audience included IOC members and representatives from 14 countries (all European with the addition of Japan). Dr Karl Evang, director-general of public health in Norway said, 'The use of dope, meaning stimulants in dope form of one kind and another, popping up here and there in the amateur sports world, needs very strong and united counter-action. If it is tolerated in any form, it will in the long run be a disaster in sports' (*New York Times*, 26 February 1952).

The American delegate to the World Health Organization, Dr Milton I. Roemer, was also concerned about the doping habit in sport. He claimed that athletes were pressurised into unhealthy practices by 'national prestige' and he criticised the intense 'competitive spirit', the 'inevitable glorification' of the athlete, and the 'commercialization' of sports. He offered a challenging view of sports' modernisation. He argued that elite sport was essentially a circus-like spectacle with the mass of the public reduced to passive spectators, and a few highly trained athletes performing 'feats of physical prowess' (*New York Times*, 26 February 1952). Doping was thus seen as part of a larger problem of sport: a small minority would entertain a demanding majority and turn to risky strategies like drug use for national and self-achievement. Such a critical view, and the linking of drugs to a wider crisis in sports, was slowly being fed into the public imagination by indignant and anxiety-ridden newspaper articles. However, Roemer took a more radical line than the later anti-doping campaigners would. This was a rare occasion when the use of drugs was linked to the very logic at the heart of competitive sport. By the time the rationale for anti-doping was firmed up in the 1960s it was the drugs – and wider social misuses of drugs – that were seen as the real culprits. Sport in its essence was considered good and pure, but drugs were like an invasion from outside, an alien external force, a plague or a cancer, that gradually ate away at the heart of sport. This is partly to do with values but also with subjective positioning: a non-sports 'outsider' might be able to criticise sports, but those working closely with athletes were more likely to try and 'manage' doping within the framework of competitive sports, not to dismantle the very thing that gave them jobs, power and prestige.

It is unclear if the concerns voiced in 1952 had any direct impact. A number of incidents in cycling had also brought the health problems to the attention of European medics, in particular the rider who died of amphetamine poisoning in 1948 at Rapallo. It was only three years after the Oslo conference that scientists in Italy were undertaking the first research into the question. Scientists working under the remit of the Italian sports medicine federation (Federazione Medico-Sportiva Italiana – FMSI) began a research project to collect empirical information about doping in April 1955 under the leadership of Antonio Venerando. He described how the group conducted 'a few sporadic analytical tests of capsules confiscated from athletes, all of which proved to have a basis of beta-phenyl-isopropylamine' (Venerando 1964: 49).[1] In the aftermath of this the FMSI took 25 urine samples during a bike race, and found five containing beta-phenyl-isopropylamine. This led to the first anti-doping Convention anywhere in the world, held in 1955 and included the FMSI and the Italian cycling federation, Unione Velocipedistra Italiana (UVI). In 1956 a cyclist was admitted to a psychiatric hospital in Montello 'his mind being deranged as a result of excessive recourse to amphetamine products'. Another admitted taking drugs and was suspended for life in 1958 after going into shock during a race 'induced by excessive recourse to sympathetico-mimetic drugs' (Venerando 1964: 49).

A number of Italian scientists were taking an interest in the issue. A first meeting was held during the 1960 Rome Olympic Games, the International Conference on Psychoergopharmacology, though available records do not reveal how much impact this meeting had. In 1961, the FMSI began working with the Italian Football Federation and a first survey of players found that 17 per cent 'were using amine substances during matches' (Venerando 1964: 48). This was followed by two round-table meetings in Florence in 1962 arranged by the FMSI. Not only was Professor Venerando actively involved but also Professors Foà, Mitolo and La Cava, all experts in sports medicine, who would eventually work with the IOC's Medical Commission. Other notable Italian scientists made their contribution:

> in May 1963, various scientific aspects of the matter were set forth in two papers read at the Convegno Nazionale di Medicina dello Sport by Professor D. Bovet, the Nobel prize winner [in 1957 for Medicine], and Professor Niccolini, a pharmacologist from Florence.
>
> (Venerando 1964: 48)

The FMSI also worked to draw up an anti-doping Convention for football, and conducted a survey of all the sports federations represented by the Italian National Olympic Committee. This showed that cycling and football were considered the most affected sports, with sporadic incidents occurring in fencing, rowing, swimming, athletics and motor-racing. An anti-doping campaign was run between July 1962 and June 1963, and the extent of doping in football fell to 1.14 per cent.

However, the fact that two cyclists were taken to hospital with amphetamine poisoning in 1962 and 1963 shows the limited influence health anxieties and testing were having on cyclists. The UVI and FMSI signed a new Convention in June 1963 to organise testing, educational programmes, and funding (Venerando 1964: 49). Tests showed that in the Italian amateur cycling championships of that year almost half of the riders were using beta-phenyl-isopropylamine. Such was the pioneering progress being made in Italy that the first definition of doping was agreed upon in Florence in 1962, one that would strongly influence the first international meeting held by the CoE committee in 1963:

> Doping is to be defined as the absorption of a substance intended to increase artificially the performance of the subject while participating in a sporting event, this being incompatible with the ethics of competition and with physical and mental integrity. The following preliminary list of prohibited substances is given to supplement this definition: (1) amphetamine and its derivatives; (2) substances similar in action to amphetamine; (3) anti-MAO[2]; (4) caffeines. It should be pointed out that these substances are not only the most commonly used, but can be easily detected.
>
> (Venerando 1964: 50)

The FMSI set up the Anti-doping Laboratory of the Sporting Medicine Centre in Florence to deal with samples, the first of its kind in the world. Any positive result would be reported to the UVI who would decide on any punishments. Antonio Venerando was President of FMSI, signatory to the Convention and clearly a key driver of these initiatives (CoE 1964). The full details of the science behind this testing are not available, however the British scientist Arnold Beckett (1986) argued that the methods used before 1965 were not sensitive enough. However, an encouraged (and overly optimistic) Antonio Venerando claimed that 'the situation seems ripe for an early and permanent solution to the doping problem on a European scale or even world-wide scale' (1964: 48).

The Italians were not alone in Europe in their efforts to establish strong anti-doping policies and strategies. The work on anti-doping by British scientists and sports policy advisors had begun as early as 1958. An interview-based survey at the 1958 Empire and Commonwealth Games showed no cases of stimulant usage, three cases of sedative usage but two of these were to help with sleep and not for competition, and substantial numbers using food supplements such as glucose and vitamins. The researchers were testing rumours that stimulants had become more popular but concluded that in 1958 the British and Commonwealth amateur competitors had not begun resorting to such measures (Fisher and Robson 1969).

The BASM had constructed a definition of doping in the early 1960s in collaboration with the British Olympic Association that was also presented to the CoE in 1963. There was an element of persuasion involved, based on a hopefulness that athletes would accept uncritically the following:

1   The only effective and safe way of ensuring optimum performance in any activity is a proper programme of training and preparation.
2   No known chemical agent is capable of producing both safely and effectively an improvement in performance in a healthy human subject.
3   Every chemical agent taken by the healthy human subject with the intention of artificially improving his performance is in some degree harmful to the individual who takes it.

(BASM 1969: 109)

After a definition of what constitutes doping, the BASM also provided a list of substances which should be banned, including alcohol, amphetamines, cocaine, narcotics, hormones and strychnine. Interestingly, hormones would be allowed if they had been used regularly for a period of 28 days or longer, and might be allowed by women who wished to suppress their menstrual period during competition (1969: 110). So we see the beginnings of an effort to classify what athletes were not allowed to take, and signs that 'cheating' was a difficult concept to pin down in practice. The point on hormones shows a complete misunderstanding that testosterone and steroids could be used over a period of time during training to build up strength and stamina. Sports medics must have been aware of the anecdotal evidence by the late 1960s given that they had been used in sports since the early 1960s.

sport', that it was 'unhealthy and contrary to the ethics of sport' (CoE 1964: 44). The ANEP initiatives were presented to IOC members through the *Bulletin du Comité International Olympique*. In an article on the subject, the very seriousness of doping was outlined along with a broad definition of practices to be banned: 'all use by absorption, injection of artificial stimulants handed before or during the competition' (1962a: 54). Even possession would lead to punishments varying from short bans, to removal of all previous wins, to lifetime bans for 'serious cases' (1962a: 54). Though there is no indication whatsoever of how the seriousness or otherwise might be established. Anti-doping ideology was outrunning policy, legal issues and the science of testing.

The other place where anti-doping was boosted by government, sports authorities and scientists was Austria. The government passed a law against doping in 1962 (Schantz 1995: 165). By 1963, the Austrian Federation of Sports Doctors had set up a Doping Commission in partnership with the sports federations and the government (CoE 1964: 27). The foremost Austrian anti-doping expert was Professor Ludwig Prokop, one of the main contributors to international anti-doping initiatives through the 1960s and 1970s. He worked with the IOC and the International Congress for Sports Sciences (ICSS) as speaker and chair of the sessions on doping at the conference hosted by Tokyo during the 1964 Olympics. He reported to the media that Knud Enemark Jensen had been using amphetamines when he died in 1960, and led some of the early testing in European cycling.

Prokop conducted a series of experiments in 1956 on a range of 'analeptics' which showed that any improvement in performance by athletes using such drugs was 'largely due to a placebo effect' (Prokop 1975:85). His initial interest in anti-doping began after seeing broken ampoules and syringes in the locker rooms of speed skaters at the 1952 Olympics, seeing a case of strychnine cramp at the 1954 Weightlifting World Championships, and 'news items concerning performance-improving drugs and different doping scandals, particularly in the international cycling field' (Prokop 1975: 85). Not only did Enemark's death seem to confirm Prokop's fears, but he witnessed further drug use by skaters at the 1964 Winter Olympics at Innsbruck. From these examples, we might surmise that Prokop was motivated by a doctor's desire to protect his patient from ill-health – he saw risky behaviour and obvious consequences, as did the Italian sports doctors and French government. And given that his experiments apparently proved the physiological ineffectiveness of drugs, we might expect his anti-doping rationalisation to focus on health.

However, this was not the case. He argued that preventing doping was 'not only in the interest of athletes' health, but also of at least equal importance is the need to try to retain the ideal of pure sporting competition and prevent sporting ideals and values from becoming falsified' (1966: 267–8). He believed that sport required all athletes to 'start under the same conditions'. And so, 'doping must be regarded primarily as a sporting and not a medical problem. Doping is unfair in any case, but not necessarily injurious to health. Doping may therefore also be regarded as a dangerous fraud' (1966: 268). In doing so, he – as with Williams and Venerando – stepped away from the physiologists of the past who argued that any substance which did not do harm could be legitimised, to argue almost the opposite case that any substance that aided performance should be banned regardless of its effect on health.

He decried the 'hardness and fanaticism' of sport, the extent to which coaches would go for victory, and the ultra-nationalism that went beyond simple prestige, 'what is intended is a documentation of the superiority of the political or economic system of the country' (1966: 268). This was a thinly veiled attack on Cold War politics, the rivalry between the USSR and the USA that turned sport (especially the Olympics) into an ideological battleground. It is enormously important to understand the individuals involved in this history, and Prokop was one of the most prominent. He seemed to be enthralled by the idealistic vision of sport as pure, noble and moral, and as a result was disappointed by corruptions of sport: drugs, politics and obsession. The elements of fair play and health began to get intertwined around this time as Prokop and other scientists who were ostensibly interested in health protection spoke and wrote about the moral virtues of sport. As such, it is clear that the social, cultural and ethical perspectives of scientists were a subtle and implicit – but enormously powerful – force in setting the framework for antidoping in the 1960s. Their traditional, paternalistic view of sport accompanied a strong faith in science as a solution to social problems. They also thought the ethics and science of anti-doping could and should be implemented in other countries: they were proselytisers as well as fanatics. It would not be long before they, and their colleagues, were using major international networks to directly influence the sporting cultures in other countries.

International Olympic Committee

The world's largest sports organisation, the IOC, was facing up to the threats of Cold War politics, professionalism and the logistical problems of hosting the Games, when the doping issue became a public controversy in the 1960s. The President, the American Avery Brundage, struggled to keep sport distant from politics and money, but the IOC was a financially weak organisation and no host had made a profit from the event since Los Angeles in 1932. The Soviet Union had entered the Games in 1952, and Brundage expressed some concern over their highly disciplined and severe system for talent development. It was highly successful, securing their place as top ranked country in almost every Summer and Winter Games between 1952 and 1988. The USA was determined to fight back and the Olympic Games came increasingly to focus tensions between two nuclear powers with ideologically opposed political and economic structures. Brundage was also interested in keeping the Olympics an amateur affair and disliked the intrusion of latent professionalism. These were testing times for the Olympics and drugs became embroiled in these complexities.

One of the first signs of concern within the IOC came in 1955, in an example which saw the doping within professional cycling impinge on the readership of the Committee's Bulletin:

In Europe this problem [doping] is being discussed more and more since it became known that the professional racing cyclist Malléjac had been doped while participating in the Tour de France. An incident which caused Mr Joinard, President of the International Cycling Union to intervene (rightly so and most judiciously) by bringing an action against an unknown party for using drugs with regard to this racing cyclist. As was to be expected, no sooner had he recovered from the evil effect of the doping, the competitor in question denied having been doped and lodged a counter-claim.

(*Bulletin du Comité International Olympique* 1955)

Five years later Brundage, in February 1960, drew members' attention to the problem of amphetamine use in certain sports (Schantz 1995). According to Arnold Beckett, 'The IOC was well aware even in 1960 of the misuse of anabolic steroids' (1991: 28). In the same month, an American academic wrote for the IOC's journal that amateurism was under threat from growing specialisation, politics and seriousness of sport. J. Kenneth Docherty worried that the acceptance of extrinsic rewards and material gain for success would 'overwhelm amateur ideals' (1960: 67). He singled out the Soviet Union and some Far East countries as presenting a challenge that needed a response. Docherty was not especially impressed by such enhancements as training, medical support, and prioritising sport over other aspects of lifestyle. He was highly critical of amphetamine use and referred directly to the AMA's 1957 critique of doping. He argued, 'it is certain that our present code of amateurism could never bless such all-out efforts' (1960: 65). This reinforced the romantic idealism popular in Olympic circles, wherein the good of sport is assumed to be true, valid and in need of protection from such 'evils' as drugs, nationalism and exploitation of athletes.

The tragic circumstances of Knud Enemark Jensen's death were a confirmation of Docherty and Brundage's anxieties. The latter saw to it that the IOC responded adequately. In the summer of 1961 he called for greater attention to the problem of doping and how it might be controlled. He also acknowledged the research being conducted by the Fédération Internationale de Médicine Sportive (FIMS) and set up a Medical Commission to contact FIMS, undertake further research, and report on possible solutions. This was headed up by Sir Arthur Porritt from New Zealand and also included Ryotaro Azuma of Japan, J. Ferreira Santos of Brazil and Josef Gruss of Czechoslovakia (Schantz 1995: 165). The idea of collecting good scientists to push forward anti-doping was gathering momentum.

The pressure was continuing to mount on the IOC, with their own journal publishing several scaremongering articles about drugs in sport. It reported problems in Swiss cycling that led to one competitor being hospitalised after using drugs, and penalties for several cyclists and their trainer (*Bulletin du Comité Internationale Olympique*, 1961). A further article highlighted the problems cycling faced since Enemark's death. There was the case in November 1960 of police raids on cyclists in Belgium that found small amounts of Benzedrine, and two Swiss cyclists having been caught with doping substances. These cases prompted the quite exaggerated opinion (note the metaphor used) that, 'One of the plagues of modern times is the disastrous practice of doping which unfortunately has been adapted to sport. The use of drugs and artificial stimulants nowadays are the chief evils from which one must protect athletes' (*Bulletin du Comité Internationale Olympique*, February 1962b: 46). According to this article, published in February 1962, the IOC contacted Professor Giuseppe La Cava, one of the Italian pioneers and now General Secretary of FIMS, 'with the view of taking action against the practice of doping ... to determine just what does and does not constitute doping' (*Bulletin du Comité Internationale Olympique*, February 1962b: 46). Three months later La Cava wrote a paper for the Bulletin discussing the problem. He focused on the 'amphetamine group' as drugs that produce such a stimulant effect that results are not a true reflection of ability and endeavour, therefore the drugs are 'illegitimate from the point of view of ethics'. Moreover, they are 'the most dangerous' from a medical perspective:

> these only apparently increase the individual's overall output, by causing the rapid and complete consumption of energy reserves through nervous stimulation. Furthermore, while they eliminate the premonitory sensations of fatigue, they do not eliminate fatigue itself or its toxins; thus the natural signal which distinguishes fatigue, a physiological phenomenon, from exhaustion, a pathological one, fails to appear, with frequently tragic consequences.
>
> (La Cava 1962: 53)

Finally, in 1963 the Bulletin summarised the report presented to the IOC at its Moscow meeting in June 1962 by J. Ferreira Santos and Mario de Carvalho Pini. Again the focus was on amphetamine-related drugs, and the call was made to the IOC, 'to take adequate measures in this combat against doping, a practice which is the very symbol of negation of the ethics of sport. This practice is growing every day and its ill-effects are felt by the human race' (Santos and Pini 1963: 57). The language used was reminiscent of the CoE's evangelising. Santos and Pini wanted 'a campaign in the world of sport in general and among the athletes in particular pointing out to them the harmful effects of doping'. And these effects were dramatically stated in what was becoming the standard 'good versus evil' terminology:

> At the present time, sport is affected by a real menace and evil: the practice of doping. It prevails in professional as well as in amateur sport. This evil must be fought. Doping provokes a false feeling of well-being which may lead the athlete to a state of auto-intoxication resulting from the physical effort he has made. It may also cause a physiological intoxication through the taking of a drug having damaging effects on the life and health of the athlete. Drugs capable of increasing the physical and mental output of the athlete artificially should certainly be prohibited.
>
> (1963: 57)

In January 1964, IOC Member for Sweden Bo Ekelund, 'disconcerted by numerous press reports of doping cases', called for the introduction of blood tests for detecting doping offenders. The man charged with taking such initiatives forward, Arthur Porritt was not for rushing this process, arguing instead that the IOC wait for his Doping Commission to report the following year (Schantz 1995: 165). When the Olympics were held in the summer of 1964 in Tokyo, a parallel event was the meeting of the ICSS, which incorporated the FIMS congress on Sports Medicine. Ludwig Prokop chaired the meeting on doping. It was proposed that FIMS accept the definition of doping and suggestions for policy implementation that came out of the Council of Europe meetings. This is unsurprising given the presence of Prokop, Dirix and Williams at all three meetings. The definition was:

> Doping is the administration to, or the use by, a competing athlete of an agent foreign to the organism by whatsoever route introduced, or of physio-logical substances in abnormal quantities or introduced by an abnormal route, with the sole intention of increasing artificially and unfair manner the performance of that subject with competition.(sic)
>
> (Kato 1964: 286)

While the IOC was well aware of the problems relating to doping, their response was slow and depended on initiatives elsewhere. There were no dedicated meetings and funding was sparse. The offer to join the 1963 CoE meetings had been declined on the basis that problems in sport should be left to sports organisations. Even when the full committee met after the 1964 Games to discuss Porritt's report, they failed to endorse even his basic requests: a declaration of anti-doping; sanctions for any national Olympic committee (NOC) or individuals who promote drug use; that NOCs should make athletes available at any time for testing; and that athletes sign a declaration that they do not use drugs and are willing to be tested (IOC 1964: 10). Moreover, there was a certain ambivalence about Prokop's view of doping drugs as presented to the 1964 sports science meeting in Tokyo:

> The placebo test possibly supplies the most convincing argument against doping. In this we were able to prove that the administration of ineffective lozenges to top athletes caused significant performance improvements, where the test persons believed them to be effective. Contrarywise, real doping medication showed scarcely any effect where it was administered as an 'ineffective' placebo. This proves the auto suggestiveness mechanism effect of most doping preparations and clearly shows the nonsense as well as the absolute uselessness of their use.
>
> (1966: 269)

This is fascinating because on one hand, it seemed the Austrian doctor was undermining anti-doping science by arguing that the drugs involved did not act in the way users imagined. At the same time though, he took part in the experimental testing conducted on cyclists during the 1964 Games. This was led by Pierre Dumas who was official doctor to the Tour de France. The tragic incidents in various races led him to investigate the sorts of substances cyclists were using during the 1962–3 season (Woodland 2003: 108–9). In 1962 an approach to the Union Cycliste Internationale (UCI) about combating doping had produced a disappointing response when the cycling governing body argued it could do nothing to prevent riders using drugs. Dumas used the platform of the conference at Uriage-les-Bains to call for more action. He followed this up by working with Albert Dirix at the 1964 Olympics alongside UCI officials and IOC advisors such as Prokop and Arnold Beckett. Prokop had first-hand experience of the attitudes riders would have to anti-doping as he faced angry response after finding amphetamines during the Tour d'Austriche in 1963. The 1964 Olympic tests involved three forms of control: a search for evidence that drugs had been injected before the race; a search of cyclists' equipment and clothing at the starting line; and urine samples. But this was a half-hearted effort and no rules had yet been established against doping. Moreover, the cyclists had been informed in advance of the tests. Albert Dirix, sports medic for the Belgian Olympic Committee, tried to make something positive from this, 'the announcement that a control will take place is effective: no traces of amphetamine were found in the urine samples taken' (1966: 184). As with the coterie of scientists he was beginning to connect with, Dirix took up a strongly moralistic stance:

> Doping has always been in the forefront among the present day problems in the field of Sports Medicine. In recent years, this evil has assumed such large proportions both within and outside the world of sport, that it seems absolutely essential to fight against it with every possible weapon; in default, we shall be faced with a problem which has certain analogies with morphomania or alcoholism.
>
> (1966: 183)

There are contradictory reports of how the cyclists responded to these drug tests. Dirix reported in 1966 that members of various national teams 'although not obliged to do so, collaborated of their own accord so as to show their willingness to co-operate' (1966: 184). He also at this time raised the fact that someone sent a letter of protest to the President of the UCI who passed it on to Avery Brundage. Perhaps this explains why Dirix wrote 22 years later that 'the task remained incomplete due to a boycott' (1988: 669). However, the slowness of response to the developing doping issue, was a reflection of leadership priorities. Allen Guttmann's biography of Avery Brundage has the following revealing point to make about the IOC's President's view on the matter:

> Although the IOC took the problem of drugs seriously and began to take measures against anabolic steroids and other agents (the first drug tests took place in Mexico City), Brundage was never as concerned about doping as he was about professionalisation. Of course he condemned the athlete who

popped pills in order to gain a competitive edge over a more sportsmanlike opponent, but drugs never seemed quite the image of evil that Mammon did.

(Guttmann 1984: 123)

Council of Europe: European bureaucracy leads the way

The meetings organised by the CoE's Out-of-School Education Committee are usually cited in doping histories because of the definition that was constructed and presented (see Houlihan 1999). However, there are other important features that need to be considered. What was the background to the meetings? Who attended them? How serious was the problem of doping considered to be? What impact did the policy have on wider international anti-doping?

As noted above, a number of countries had already established anti-doping regulations and were beginning to modernise this through testing and surveying. There were national-level collaborations between sports federations and sport medicine organisations. This was an emerging collaborative enterprise, which has previously been underestimated, as Barrie Houlihan, describing the pre-1963 efforts wrote: 'Until the mid 1960s, concerns about doping had been limited to a relatively small group of specialists within sport and the private concern had not yet become a public issue' (1999: 130). However, there was clearly a great deal of pressure on specific sports federations which led them to seek help from medical, legal and administrative experts. That pressure was partly the result of the increased media emphasis on the critical aspects of drug use. As J. G. P. Williams noted, 'Somewhat surprisingly, in view of the volume of sensational publicity given to the doping of athletes, published material available to the [CoE] working party was rather limited' (1963: 39). It is ironic that much of this publicity was based on Ludwig Prokop's mistaken 'interpretation' of the events leading to Knud Enemark Jensen's death in 1960 (Møller 2005).[3] The CoE report itself does not identify any specific event leading up to the 1963 meetings though it is claimed that many cases of extensive physical and psychological damage, including fatalities, have been proven. However, the evidence shows that the matter of sports doping had suddenly become transformed. No longer were the abstract musings of the likes of Adolphe Abrahams suitable for such a serious topic, they had been replaced by a much more forceful ideology:

> All participants attach great importance to European co-operation in stamping out the doping of athletes, which they regard as a social evil having ramifications far beyond the realm of sport ... Experience shows that in those sports in which doping is already prevalent, the moral and physical consequences of the practice have already begun to undermine the whole structure of the sport. If doping is allowed to grow unchecked, the time will come when all the benefits accruing to the individual and to the community from the practice of sport will be lost.

(CoE, 1964: 4–5)

The first meeting included 14 delegates representing Austria, Belgium, France, Italy, the Netherlands, Spain, Switzerland, Sweden, Turkey and the UK. The majority were experts in sports medicine. The second meeting was no larger in terms of geographical coverage or numbers and indeed included many of the same individuals. The summary of these individuals' responses to the CoE questionnaire shows that doping was treated differently across Europe. Only Austria, for instance, had a national law against doping while that of France was being prepared at this time. Some countries, but not all, had established strong relationships between sports and medical organisations. However, there was also a divergence of opinion as to the extent of the doping issue. J. G. P. Williams – Britain's sole representative – stated that, 'Doping is not a serious problem in the United Kingdom' (CoE 1964: 32). Though he did later reflect in the 1962–3 period in a different way, arguing that surveys of individual competitors in various sports had shown 'the occasional use of more or less powerful dopes'; and that the problem lay with the national governing bodies in Britain who 'with one exception all denied that doping occurred in their sport, nearly all stated that they did not legislate against it and none had ever carried out any tests or controls' (Williams 1969: 128).

Between these representatives a problem which was slowly gaining recognition in a few countries was promoted to a matter of much grander proportions and greater urgency. It was argued that doping presented a hidden danger, 'The public at large is frequently ignorant of the gravity of the problem' (CoE 1964: 4). These were created by the pressures of commercialism and national prestige:

> The intensity of competition in sport at both domestic and international levels and the increasingly disproportionate social and economic rewards of success have resulted in greater efforts of all kinds to improve physical performance ... such methods include the use of various pharmacological agents and psychological procedures to improve performance artificially, the practice known as doping.
>
> (CoE 1964: 5)

Moreover, 'Drug-taking and other methods of stimulation by athletes have implications going beyond the sphere of sport: medical, moral, legal, social and commercial' (CoE 1964: 4). As noted previously, this was a period when a problem that could have been defined and managed as one of a number of heath-associated issues in sport, was made into something much grander: a moral panic that played on deeper social anxieties. The 'terrors of the social subconscious' (Kohn 1992: 2) were being voiced.

The solutions offered played into the hands of those who contributed towards and wrote this policy: more medical research, more conferences, and more responsibility to the European bureaucracies. As such, two other conferences were held in 1963, one in France and the other in Brazil (probably due to the presence of Pini). And it was argued that, 'The European community is particularly well endowed with the specialised technological, judicial and medical *savoir-faire* to abolish the practice of doping and thus protect its own people and give a lead to the world' (CoE 1964: 5). Anti-doping experts wanted to extend their ideas across the world: the CoE presented, in the name of international co-operations, a remarkably ethnocentric, arrogant and pseudo-imperialistic perspective. They were suggesting that the European models for modernity and progress combined with current expertise can solve this problem across the world, and change the cultural attitudes of other populations. In effect, the doping debate was reformulated so that it was no longer about health but also about morality, and it was expected that the rest of the world would come to view the morality of doping according to the guidelines set out in Europe. Governmental or commercial interests must not, it was argued, take precedence over the health of young athletes. The consequences were stated in almost Biblical terms, 'Apathy of the part of those morally responsible is a crime against humanity' (CoE 1964: 6). Perhaps it was no coincidence that most of the countries represented were Catholic and all were Christian. There was something subtly religious about this idea of protecting young people from the pressures of modern life, a desire to return to traditional values, almost to simpler pre-modern times. There was a frequent recourse to morality, and a desire to make physical recreation and competition take on all manner of moral values and symbolism. It was through this document that doping became routinely described as an evil, indeed the first section of the second report is entitled 'Fighting an Evil', and Good is clearly represented by anti-doping science and policy. The demand for social reform under the guise of good grace and pseudo-religious benevolence echoes European histories of imperialism and belies fundamental fears over secular processes of change. As Antonio Venerando wrote:

> doping, like any other form of drug addiction or contagious disease, cannot be eradicated in one country alone; it must be fought steadily, with equal pertinacity and determination, in all other countries as well. In Europe at least, and more particularly among the nations of common Latin origin, the anti-doping campaign should be given practical form as rapidly as possible, and be translated from words into action. The Italian experience can be of great value here, facilitating the immediate practical results which are needed to avoid the risk of further damage and unethical victories won by fraud. Young people will then return to sport with unblemished aims, competing by fair means and restoring to sport its primary function as a means of preparation for life itself.
>
> (1964: 53)

This echoed Ludwig Prokop's underlying ideology when he claimed that concerted anti-doping efforts 'should result in effective protection against the immoral act of doping. Thus we shall be able to continue to keep the ideal of sports pure, for the welfare of all mankind' (1964: 269). It is no wonder doping was forced underground and that suspicion fell on those who failed to prove their innocence.

Conclusion

Anti-doping was born in the mid 1950s. The impetus came from medical author-ities looking on from outside sport, observing the excesses, and worrying about the influence of drug use and addiction on public health. The wider social con-text was one of increasing anxiety and governmental legislation across the developed world.

However, there was a time when the use of amphetamine drugs could have been legitimised and openly discussed. Up until the late 1950s, and in some quar-ters until the late 1960s, athletes were unhindered by too much ethical baggage to prevent them turning to such drugs for performance enhancement. The seri-ousness of the AMA's intervention in 1957 shows that health was increasingly becoming a major factor in discussions of drugs in sport. By the time of the CoE's policy in 1963, there was a second factor built in to anti-doping discourse: sports-manship. What would become of the twin pillars of anti-doping were essentially social constructs of the late 1950s and early 1960s. This was therefore a pivotal historical moment, one that changed forever the way we think about sports dop-ing. It had a series of unintended consequences, including making amphetamines appear useful for performance and forcing athletes to find other drugs if amphet-amines were being tested for. The task of anti-doping was handed over to scientists who viewed the problem in a modernist rational-bureaucratic way, assuming that better science and more testing would solve the problem. These were backed up by a pseudo-religious rhetoric that set good against evil, with the good protecting the youth of the world from the evil of doping.

One of the complicating factors of this period was that anti-doping authority was largely in the hands of scientists. As a consequence anti-doping was charac-terised by faith in rational argument and faith in the power of science to enforce policy. That may be why such a strong pseudo-religious rhetoric underpinned the early campaigning to stop doping. And also why such a black-and-white approach was taken: there was no scope for reduced dosages or medical supervision of drug use or advice to drug takers. Athletes were either clean or they were guilty, they were good or evil, there was no middle ground and no scope for ethical dilemmas.

However, even individual scientists such as Ludwig Prokop seemed to operate within a certain ambiguity. They set out to persuade athletes and coaches that drugs such as amphetamines firstly would have no effective impact on perfor-mance and secondly would lead to a range of health problems. At the same time, without making it explicit, they knew this strategy was likely to fail, and so set about the science of testing with greater enthusiasm. It was almost like saying: if we can't talk them out of it we'll catch and punish them. If they don't listen to reason they will face the consequences. And so denial coexisted with testing. Highlighting the negative health effects was the most realistic form of propa-ganda, athletes might be dissuaded from indulging if they knew the risks. However, even that seems patronising and weak if the scientists did not enter into any dialogue with athletes or seek to understand their perspective. More problematic was the strategy of denying efficacy as athletes and their entourage had experience, anecdotes and suspicion about their competitors' drug use, to balance against anything a doctor might tell them. And if the scientists really believed the drugs didn't work, then why bother constructing a framework of regulation, education, testing and punishment? Athletes probably deduced that if a drug was deserving of such status to be on the list of banned substances it was more than likely to be a useful aid to performance. The more the authorities pushed their twin strategies of denial and testing, the more sensible it seemed to try out some of these drugs. It was like telling a 10-year-old not to eat candy.

Perhaps aware of their weak position or genuinely motivated by idealism, the group of scientists that included Prokop, Dirix, Dumas, Beckett and Williams, put forward a fundamentalist view of ethics and a pseudo-imperialist strategy of moral diffusion. Supported by the modernist techniques of surveillance, testing, policy and punishment, anti-doping experts enhanced their mechanisms of power. The body was fast becoming the focal point for competing ideologies and tensions within the same organisations. Purity and ethics were imposed from above while athletes continued to pursue their competitive instincts regardless of the paternalistic advice.

7 Science, morality and policy
The modernisation of anti-doping, 1965–1976

Introduction

While the moral views on doping were gathering pace by the early 1960s, the science was only beginning to catch up. The desire to stop doping and penalise 'cheats' needed a supporting mechanism as athletes could not be trusted to subsume their will to win for the sake of fair play idealism. As the previous chapter has detailed, a small number of scientists in continental Europe had begun developing a test for amphetamine use, namely Antonio Venerando and his colleagues in Italy, and Pierre Dumas, Albert Dirix and Ludwig Prokop in the 1964 Olympic Games. The cultural context for these changes was very specific: changing social perceptions of the value of science and technology; anxieties over drug use in youth cultures; professionalism and nationalism in sport; the modernising rational-scientific approach to sports performance; the rising profile of sports stars in the media. At the same time, a number of newspaper journalists were beginning to realise that drugs provided scandal and a story. The exposé of Everton players using amphetamines illustrates this point.

This chapter deals with the highly important and influential period when science, morality and policy came together to modernise the anti-doping strategy at international level. This required the collective efforts of individual researchers and governing bodies. In particular, this story depends upon the initiatives of a group of scientists in London feeding into the growing clamour among IOC members to ensure the Olympics were 'clean'. This was a heady mix of British traditions of science and fair play in sport working alongside European bureaucracy and fantasies of amateurism enshrined in the idea of Olympism. By 1965 British scientists had refined the testing procedure for amphetamines and run official tests in that year's Tour of Britain cycle race and the 1966 football World Cup in England, leading directly to the first Olympic testing in 1968.

The other facilitating process was the unstoppable and dangerous use of amphetamines by professional cyclists. This had been identified by Dirix, Venerando, Dumas, Prokop and others. However, police efforts and testing in the early 1960s were resisted by cyclists. By the middle of the decade top riders such as Jacques Anquetil were making public statements in favour of doping, and in 1966 the Tour de France competitors staged a 'go-slow' in protest against anti-doping measures.

Everything changed in 1967. The death of Englishman Tommy Simpson during the Tour de France meant that amphetamine use could no longer be tolerated. In the same year, the IOC established its Medical Committee chaired by Prince Alexandre de Merode, and the BASM hosted a major international conference on the subject. By the early 1970s, the problem of steroid use was being addressed by British researchers, and another conference was hosted by the British Association of Sports Medicine in 1975. From the end of the 1960s and into the 1970s, the IOC faced increasing criticism for failing to protect the Games from doping. The new President, Lord Killanin, argued that doping could spell the end of international sporting competition. The seriousness of the threat was beginning to dawn on the world's governing bodies, but usage among Western and Eastern bloc athletes continued apace. The introduction of a test for steroids at the 1976 Games did not stop doping. However, it did allow policy rules to be established and did lead eventually to a raft of positive tests. It ended a hundred years of relatively open drug use, and ushered in a new period of deceit, underground innovation, high profile 'catches', and difficult decisions on borderline drugs.

Refining the amphetamine test

Prior to the issue of doping becoming a major public issue, indeed from 1958, Professor Arnold Beckett and his colleagues at the Chelsea College, London, had been working on methods to find trace amounts of drugs and metabolites in biological fluids. In March 1965 they presented a paper focusing on amphetamines at the International Research Symposium on Medicinal Chemistry at Chelsea College. During the conference, Beckett was approached by a Belgian scientist, Dr Paul Janssen, who was interested in sports applications. The key elements were timing and reliability. Janssen was apparently encouraged when Beckett told him the results could be known in 48 hours. Beckett later reported that Janssen's idea was to 'notify sports authorities of our important sensitive methods because in many countries a very serious problem of drug misuse in sport was developing' (Beckett 1986: 564). It became clear that the techniques being implemented by Venerando and colleagues in Italy, and Dumas and colleagues at the 1964 Olympics, were inadequate because results from laboratories were being returned as negative 'even when it was known generally that competitors being tested were using drugs' (Beckett 1986: 564).

This accidental meeting of individuals sharing a common research interest, but one with an awareness of sports problems in mainland Europe, led to the development of refined tests. The initial procedure of gas chromatography was used to find a number of closely related amines. But Beckett's group had a deeper knowledge, for instance, of how to deal with variances in the metabolism of a drug. As he wrote, 'if methylamphetamine is given, then one must find both the drug and its metabolite, amphetamine' (Beckett 1986: 565). Moreover, they developed awareness of how different conditions of drug ingestion and excretion could be measured and tested. Very soon, a better analytical method called mass spectrometry was introduced. This was applied at the Tour of Britain in that year, leading to three disqualifications, and it was put to use at the 1966 World Cup (Beckett *et al.* 1966). This time there were no positives. However, accuracy of the procedure was ensured as Beckett and his team found 'very small amounts of bases in urine and it was established subsequently that these had arisen from the use of certain nasal drops by some competitors' (1986: 566).

The English Football Association worked closely with the Chelsea College laboratory to establish precise, secure mechanisms to prevent any form of tampering. A random test was undertaken at every match, decided by ballot though the referee was also given scope to select any player for a drugs test. The system for collecting the sample and ensuring safe delivery to the laboratory was detailed and aimed towards infallibility and anonymity. The testing was done within six hours and observed by an independent witness. Such was the success of the procedures that the official tournament report stated:

> Apart from the two instances [of nasal spray causing a positive result], all of the other tests proved negative, and the consensus of opinion is that no better deterrent to the possibility of doping could have been devised ...This anti-doping operation was carried out with clockwork precision, even though the system had to be devised at very short notice.
>
> (Mayes 1967: 78)

It is quite astounding that the system of collecting a sample, separating it into two bottles, labelling them with codes to ensure anonymity, verifying that they could not be tampered with, was quickly put together but set the format for sample collection for the rest of the century.

As one of the leading experts who consolidated the science of anti-doping, Beckett's views on the reasons for anti-doping are important elements of this history. He was as interested in the social as much as the health factors. He cited three reasons: to protect those athletes given drugs without their consent; the risks to competitors and spectators from aggression and loss of judgement caused by drugs; and the role model argument, that awareness of athletes' transgressions 'would have devastating effects on young people as a whole' (1986: 569). As noted in Chapter 6, the BASM already had an influential definition and policy statement by 1962, and Williams went to the CoE meetings in 1963 and the Tokyo conference in 1964. As such, we can see that British scientists had an important part to play in the early initiatives. However, Beckett's role proved the catalyst to a deepening of interest and influence in the UK. As will be shown, this led eventually to a number of conferences and developments in finding a test for steroids in the early 1970s. But the event that reinforced British commitment and prominence was the conference held in 1967 by the BASM that brought international experts to London whose papers were published in the *British Journal of Sports Medicine* in 1969.

Sports medicine and morality in Britain

The conference included three of the British experts who were pushing forward anti-doping science at the international level: J. G. P. Williams, Arthur Porritt and Arnold Beckett. It was Porritt who opened the symposium with a wide-ranging overview of the situation. Even by this stage, the use of anabolic steroids was seen as a fringe element while 'it is mostly the members of the amphetamine group in one form or another that are the main cause for concern' (1969: 106). He explained that the rise of drug use was the result of 'heavily intensified competition ... the importance of national prestige ... and the very greatly increased rewards for sport for professionals and, regrettably, amateurs as well' combined with 'a frightfully rapid development in the pharmacological field' (1969: 106). He outlined the common view of health risks: removal of the natural signs of fatigue; problems with co-ordination and judgement; and addiction.

The 'moral implications' were those related to 'sportsmanship' and 'fair competition' but interestingly the reason why drugs would undermine these is because they would not be available to all the competitors. Porritt suggested education coming from the medical profession and regulations by sports authorities. Finally, he acknowledged 'the religious aspects' as 'it is a moral problem in which the leaders of various churches could help the medical profession and all social workers very greatly. So far this primary field has been virtually neglected' (1969: 108). This may be the only effort to explicitly link doping, morality and religion even though the subtle, implicit and perhaps subconscious ways in which religion informed anti-doping are much more frequent. In other writings, Porritt's ideological constructs were informed by a dichotomous sense of morality and paternalistic responsibility, 'Doping is an evil – it is morally wrong, physically dangerous, socially degenerate and legally indefensible' (1965: 166). He thought doping reflected a 'weakness of character', that it was a 'temptation, in this fast-moving dynamic and somewhat amoral world in which we live today' and thus controls should be in place (1965: 167). Interestingly he also hoped such 'emergency' controls would be 'temporary' (1965: 167) – a passing comment that, given later events, was naïve and hopelessly optimistic.

However, there was still no consensus on this issue. Another contributor to the symposium, M. Hollyhock, argued that 'the use of amphetamine or the anabolic steroids for limited periods, under strict supervision, is unlikely to be harmful in a person who is physically and psychologically normal' (1969: 126). Neither was fair play seen as a strong anti-doping argument, 'it is not clear as to how it is intrinsically unfair. The use of drugs is no more unfair in one sense than the fact that one athlete will have a good coach and excellent training facilities whereas another does not' (1969: 126). Moreover, if the rules were open enough, Hollyhock saw no difference between using stimulants to improve performance and a team making substitutions during a game to improve their play. He concluded by suggesting that in times of peace patriotic fervour is focused on sport. And so, 'a situation in which the competitive urges of thousands of spectators are vicariously resolved to a few performers must put those performers under the kind of pressure which will often submerge the enjoyment of the sport for its own sake' (1969: 127). Drug use may well follow, and Hollyhock offered a critical view of sport itself, not just the risky activity of doping, 'It is really impossible to isolate dope in the context of modern sport – it is simply but one of a number of facets in a wider and more intriguing problem' (1969: 127). It appears that such critical views of sport were not taken seriously by audiences consisting of former athletes, members of sports governing bodies, or sports doctors. To suggest that it was sport itself, rather than the drugs, that was essentially unfair and unhealthy, was to swim against the tide and risk professional status.

These discussions reveal certain frank differences in opinion. No contributor argued in favour of doping, but it was obvious that drawing lines between legal and illegal, finding ways to catch cheats, getting athletes and their coaches on board, or even organising international sports authorities, was going to be highly demanding. A number of British individuals played a key role in this, despite the fact that British athletes were seen as comparatively innocent. Indeed, Williams argued that doping is not 'proportionally' a 'very big' problem and that 'with the encouragement of what has been achieved already, it is possible to feel with some confidence that British sport will be spared the disaster of widespread and uncontrolled doping' (1969: 133).

It appears that many British authority figures felt responsible, not just for ensuring that their own country could appear 'clean' but that others were protected from the various negative consequences of doping. There was a strong sense that fair play should continue to be a feature of modern sport. R. H. Raynes, a public health specialist argued that the doped athlete 'is cheating, and persistent cheating may be the first step towards a progressive moral degradation' (1969: 150). Perhaps just as important was the wider social scene of drug use in Britain which had changed rapidly since the conservative 1950s and caused much conflict between the moral/legal movement for regulation and the demands of self-indulgent, experimental, free-living, youth cultures. Fisher and Robson reflected on the changes in sport and society from a more innocent period:

> Outside sport, in 1958, the problem of teenage doping in Britain had not yet come to the fore; the pop groups were only just beginning to set national trends among the youth, and the almost open market of pep pills, purple hearts and even narcotics through the coffee bars, strip clubs and 'love-ins' was not yet established ... Within a few years drug taking spread in Britain, and a black market for pep pills was soon established. Drugs that offset fatigue in all-night jive and rock sessions could easily be tried out to offset fatigue in sport, and be found efficacious ... the general permissiveness of society does little to discourage youngsters, whether competing in sport or not, to seek new thrills and experiences.
>
> (1969: 164–5)

The British attitude generally around the late 1960s and into the 1970s was one of commitment to anti-doping. Regular articles in newspapers outlined the potential health risks of steroids and the threat to fair play values. Even when testing was introduced in an experimental way at the 1970 Commonwealth Games in Edinburgh, there was uproar that any positives could not be punished:

> Lieutenant Colonel Fraser, the medical superintendent at the competitors' village, has confirmed that no action will be taken if it is proven that an athlete has broken international sports rules by taking steroids, and no names of those sinning will be revealed. This seems an extraordinary decision and Mr Wally Holland, manager of the English weightlifting team, said yesterday that he was flabbergasted that such infringements should ever be tolerated.
>
> (*The Times*, 17 July 1970)

This does seem quite presumptuous given that the IOC did not ban steroids until 1974 when a reliable test had been found. Indeed, the major studies in this field were not published until 1974 and 1975. (It is not entirely clear who conducted these tests and using what sort of methods.) Nonetheless, the comments by Holland and the emotive position taken up by *The Times* newspaper indicates that the established, majority opinion in Britain was against doping. By 1972 such headlines as 'Drugs put British athletes' health at risk' (*The Times*, 21 April 1972) show the consensus of opinion and the scaremongering tactics of authoritarian discourses. Indeed the health risks of steroid use were regularly cited in media stories despite a lack of scientific evidence to support such claims, perhaps symbolising the weakness of the fair play rationale for anti-doping.

Such was the British interest in the subject that the BASM hosted a second major international conference, this time entitled 'Anabolic Steroids and Sport' and published the proceedings in the *British Journal of Sports Medicine*. By this time, Arthur Porritt was a Peer of the Realm and President of BASM. The journal Editorial noted that:

> In the past few years, developments in complicated biomedical techniques, increasing awareness of the hazards of overdosage of hormones, and a spread of the use of steroids by athletes, have justified this Association in organising another symposium on doping, this time devoted to the use, abuse and detection of anabolic steroids in sport.
>
> (BASM 1975a: 58)

Much of the conference was devoted to highly technical studies of the effects of steroids and the construction of a testing system. But the British attitude of despair, that drugs ruined sport, was best represented by A. H. Payne, who drew the conference's attention to some of the hypocrisies in anti-doping:

> Sport for all? I don't think that sport is for the top class athlete. There is this paradox that the top end of sport is nothing like it is lower down. Perhaps the ladder of progress goes through the clouds and enters some cuckoo land where, whatever it is we do it is something other than sport. In the narrow context of

the symposium we are concerned about sport and sport should be synonymous with fair play. But there isn't fair play when some are aided by drugs. Are we to ensure that everyone has access to these drugs in order to ensure fair play – or do we admit that the title of this symposium is a contradiction in terms? ... Are the rest of us, the general public, not encouraging the athlete to cheat when we agree with the reporter who writes of that athlete's failure in an unfair competition? Or is that non-drugged loser the real 'winner' after all?

(1975: 88)

The pragmatic line taken by most interested parties was that sport needed to continue but the authorities had to clamp down on drug use. Suggestions that deeper problems needed to be solved first were ignored. Perhaps the best comparison is with alcohol use, where the deeper social problems that lead to addiction, that is homelessness, poverty, stressful domestic relations, macho cultures of binge drinking, have not been tackled by the punitive strategies such as banning drink-drivers. Nonetheless, British individuals were pushing forward anti-doping through media coverage, conferences and scientific research. Most significantly, the British sports establishment led the way in trying to find an accurate and applicable method for steroid testing.

The science of testing

Arguably, the role of scientists is the great omission in the current historiography of doping and anti-doping. There has been some confusion on this matter, even in such supposedly expert places as the CoE's 1989 Anti-Doping Convention:

> In the 1970s, action was taken by several national sports organisations (for example, in the Federal Republic of Germany, by the *Deutscher Sportbund;* in Norway by the Norwegian Confederation of Sport) and most of the international sports federations involved in the Olympic Games aligned their own regulations on those which they had to follow when at the Olympic Games. But if procedures slowly improved, so also did doping techniques: the ingestion of anabolic steroids to increase muscle mass and endurance; the use of peptide hormones (for example HCG) and the application of testosterone to improve strength/weight ratios. There were rumours of the use of blood-doping in endurance events, and news of the abuse of substances and procedures multiplied considerably in the late 1970s. The pioneering work into detection and analysis techniques undertaken at the first IOC-recognised laboratories, particularly the one at Cologne, financed by the Government of the Federal Republic of Germany, provided evidence of large-scale and often sophisticated abuse. Competitors were being encouraged to win – by friends, by their entourage – on the basis of rumours of success, and thinking they would be unlikely to be tested, or if so, not detected.

(CoE 1989: 3)

The major gap in the above is the work of other scientists who helped discover the first test for steroids in the early 1970s. In 1971 Avery Brundage asked Alexandre de Merode if the IOC's Medical Commission had found a method for detecting hormones. De Merode's answer shows where he thought the best work was being done, 'Prince de Merode replied that Professor Beckett of Great Britain, had studied this subject and was the most eminent world specialist. However, he had not gone far enough in his research for the Medical Commission to use any control in this field' (IOC 1971).

The first evidence of funding for this research comes from British media reports that Professor F. T. G. Prunty of St. Thomas' Hospital had been given grant funding by the Sports Council to find a method of detecting steroids (*The Times*, 21 April 1972), though as noted above, there was some form of experimental testing carried out at the 1970 Commonwealth Games in Edinburgh. There was certainly a broad movement in Britain to condemn the use of these drugs. The Sports Council had only been established in 1972 so it seems that one of their first tasks was to support Prunty's research. Elsewhere, the British Association of National Coaches (BANC) spoke out against the drugs (*The Times*, 14 October 1972), Beckett, Williams and Lucking were joined by Arthur Gold and Roger Bannister in the fight against doping. Beckett approached Professor Raymond Brooks who also worked in London, to suggest he also worked on developing a test. It is not clear if and how Prunty and Brooks made any connection though they did work in the same hospital. Beckett (1976) himself does not mention Prunty's efforts when outlining this history, instead pointing to key studies by Brooks *et al.* (1975) and Ward *et al.* (1975).

The technical details of the science were much more complicated than the amphetamine tests. The important breakthrough came with the availability of radioimmunoassay techniques which were highly sensitive (Brooks *et al.* 1975); while Sumner (1974) was responsible for developed antisera 'with the desired specificity for certain characteristic features of various types of anabolic steroids' (Beckett 1976: 596); and Ward *et al.* (1975) used a gas chromatographic-mass spectrometric method for finding a parent drug and its metabolites in urine after the positive result was given by the radioimmunoassay method (Beckett 1976). These were highly important shifts in scientific knowledge that could, in theory, reverse the trend of doping-enhanced performances. The earliest trial run was held during the 1974 Commonwealth Games in New Zealand. Of the 55 samples in the trial, nine failed the radioimmunoassay test, with seven confirmed to be positive by the gas chromatographic-mass spectrometric method (Kicman and Gower 2003). The IOC's response was to put anabolic steroids on the list of banned substances in April 1974, just two months after this successful trial run of the two forms of testing (Kicman and Gower 2003: 323).

However, Beckett knew in 1976 that the testing was inevitably going to be flawed:

> A competitor may take anabolic steroids during training, then discontinue their use two to three weeks before a particular event; a urine sample collected

at the event may not show a positive result even though the competitor may still be having an advantage at least in weight from the drug misuse.

(1976: 597)

Nonetheless, perhaps in the hope of finding solutions to such problems, the IOC Medical Commission banned the use of steroids in 1974. Beckett was surprised given that 'at the time the gas liquid chromatographic/mass spectrometric methods had not been developed sufficiently' (1976: 597). So, as a direct consequence of Brooks' discovery in 1975 and the associated research fed into IOC policy:

> In April 1975, the IOC Medical Commission designated the radioimmunoassay as a screening test only, and gas liquid chromatographic/mass spectrometry evidence to establish unequivocally the structure of the steroid used was made mandatory. It was agreed that testing for anabolic steroids must be carried out for the 1976 Olympic Games in Montreal.
>
> (1976: 597)

The IOC were thus the first major sports authority to implement the new test, however, it had been a long road and not without some controversy.

The International Olympic Committee

While the sad events of summer 1967 in France proved something of a watershed in cycling, the IOC was making moves that would change the face of the global fight against doping. The Medical Commission was established under the chairmanship of Prince Alexandre de Merode. The definition of doping was accepted as 'the use of substances or techniques in any form or quantity alien or unnatural to the body with the exclusive aim of obtaining an artificial or unfair increase in performance in competition' (cited in Beamish and Ritchie 2004: 361). In May 1967 Sir Arthur Porritt presented a summary of his report that had taken almost five years to complete; the lack of urgency does not reflect many of the IOC members' concerns. He argued in favour of enhancing the 'medical machinery to cope with these problems' and constructed a list of banned substances which read briefly, 'Alcohols, Amphetamines and Ephedrine, Cocaine, Vasodilators, Opiates, Cannabis' with a further note that 'the use of Anabolic Steroids (except for medical purposes) constitutes "doping" from an Olympic viewpoint' (IOC 1967). The list was regarded by Porritt as 'not exhaustive', a strangely unscientific approach which perhaps hoped to use the spirit of anti-doping rulings as a guide without needing the absolute fixedness of a specific and comprehensive list.

At the same time, Porritt presented a summary of steroid use by the British doctor and former shot-putter Martyn Lucking. He listed the products available and noted they 'have been increasingly used in sport since at least 1963'. They would be effective at building muscle in conjunction with a high protein diet and muscle strengthening exercises thus bringing 'obvious advantages'. However, Lucking admitted that finding a test would be 'difficult' especially as steroids were used widely in training rather than in competition. Developing a test would require 'close co-operation with an expert endocrinologist with specialised laboratory facilities', specifically the 'most informed department' in Britain was that headed by Professor Prunty at St Thomas' Hospital, London. He mentioned the health issues but played them down by claiming that 'the harmful effects are few'. Such a view may not have done much to persuade IOC members that action on this issue was urgent. Certainly, the focus remained on amphetamines and on gender testing at least until an adequate test for steroids could be developed.

There was a growing unease about the ways in which sport was changing, essentially about the modernisation rapidly implemented by some countries towards what Beamish and Ritchie call 'the most extreme manifestations of the forces of scientific rationality and the cult of victory that increasingly threatened to undermine and debase the Olympic project' (2004: 361). De Merode presented the results of the Medical Commission's first meetings to the IOC's Executive Board in January 1969. The strategy was three-pronged: first, they established rules that excluded athletes who had 'been shown to use dope', and if relevant, also the team they represented, and any athlete who failed to attend the dope control; second, they established controls 'according to the most modern and appropriate methods'; and third, a list of banned products which at this stage included amphetamines, ephedrine and similar substances, central nervous stimulants such as strychnine and analeptics, narcotics and analgesics, antidepressants and tranquillisers (IOC 1969a). This is curiously vague and a trifle naïve: the idea of 'similar substances' might be used by either party to defend their position. Athletes could have used solucamphre, caffeine, testosterone or anabolic steroids and argue they were not breaking any rules. Moreover, the IOC had not only taken out the reference to steroids made by Porritt two years earlier but his inclusion of alcohol and cannabis was also considered superfluous. The problems with the list of banned substances were evident from the beginning. Sex testing was also introduced at this time, with the IOC making firm connections between the problem of gender ambivalence and the use of performance-enhancing drugs (Ritchie 2003).

One result from the dope testing showed what controversy could ensue. A member of the Swedish pentathlon team in the 1968 Games was found to have 'too great an amount of alcohol in their system' leading to the disqualification of the whole team. Three medals were subsequently returned by the Swedes to the IOC (IOC 1969b). However, alcohol was not specifically mentioned on the list of banned substances though could in theory be part of the antidepressants category. No guidelines or rules were given on legal limits. In later, more litigious days, imposing such sanctions on the basis of such vague definitions would not have been accepted. More pertinently, a raft of other evidence has shown that amphetamines and steroids were being widely used by the time of the 1968 Games. The fact that the only 'positive' was for alcohol shows up the testing system as laughable. By the late 1960s, the rules and the morality were in place but the science was struggling to keep up. The long time IOC member and now head of the World Anti-Doping Agency (WADA), Dick Pound has criticised this period by arguing that 'one of the fundamental mistakes made by the IOC in the doping field was to leave the leadership in the hands of scientists rather than generalists' (2004: 57). Another criticism has been that the IOC tried to devolve responsibility to lower level organisations – national governing bodies or international sports federations – that could not be trusted to police themselves (Hoberman 2005). Certainly, Brundage made it clear in the late 1960s that 'although the general arrangements for the testing should be put up by the IOC Medical Commission, the actual responsibility should remain with the International Federations' (IOC 1968). This mixture of narrowing the paradigm within which anti-doping worked, and passing on responsibility meant that the more fundamental issues about how sport was changing were not being addressed seriously.

In an attempt to do so, however, in 1970 the German Dr Georg van Opel presented a written paper to the IOC on 'The Future of Sport' (IOC 1970a). His polemical thesis centred on the destruction of sporting idealism due to professionalism, obsession with records, institutionalised training regimes and nationalism:

> There is no longer any room at the Olympic Games for the development of free individuality and for contests among free persons. The political comparison of nations in the sportsfield has brought about by force the transformation of the lover of sport (amateur) into the national athlete and puppet in the struggle of power politics. The step-by-step adaptation to the national passion for self-assertion in sport is the gradual loss of freedom and human dignity in sport. The national athlete is an agent commission by the state, a man enslaved by his mission, a manipulable tool of the state and propaganda. The national athlete must train and must win.
>
> (1970a: 88)

Emotions were clearly running high in some quarters as the Olympics became increasingly wrapped up with Cold War politics. The USSR had institutionalised sporting excellence with the support of the government; the USA responded with determined efforts to match and even surpass their successes. Through the 1960s the 'drama of a no-holds-barred athletic confrontation between the two super powers was the direct antithesis of de Coubertin's lofty aspirations for the revived Games' (Beamish and Ritchie 2004: 359). Brundage worked hard to defend de Coubertin's principles and to protect the idealism that was so intertwined with amateurism. Van Opel appealed for an end to the Olympic Movement altogether if the trend toward professionalism – and the death of the amateur – continued unabated. He did admit, however, that most athletes, sport authorities and political governments were in favour of the continuing modernisation of sport towards scientific, nationalistic and commercial ends. He deplored this as the degeneration of sport, as 'deadly serious', and attacked the system of talent development and sensationalism that was out of proportion with its importance, 'the thousands of millions sacrificed for victories threaten to make slaves of athletes and they are suitable to be used in a roundabout way to finance sensations, while one third of humanity is starving' (1970a: 94).

The IOC members hardly acknowledged van Opel's broadside. They certainly did not discuss abandoning the Olympics or even challenging the rapid modernisation that was happening in elite sports. They were unlikely to as Brundage's 'interpretation of the athlete as an isolated-hero-in-torment influenced him to see sport as an absolute experience, analogous to religion, which had to be protected from contamination at all costs' (Hoberman 1986: 53). There had been a sharp rise in training methods, time devoted to training, involvement of coaches and medics, and the use of various legal and illegal performance-enhancing techniques. The response was to treat the symptoms but not the cause. So in 1970 a decision was made to publish a pamphlet ahead of the Winter and Summer Games of 1972 that would provide details of doping rules and testing procedures for athletes and coaches (IOC 1970a). Even such a small gesture prompted concerns among members about the costs involved in organising anti-doping (IOC 1970b). While van Opel's concerns were entirely ignored, various obstacles were being put in the way of those fighting drug abuse in the Games. The financial cost of organising the lab during the Munich Games of 1972 was brought to the members' attention as it came in at a quite significant $1.5m (IOC 1973).

Nonetheless, the anti-doping rules were included in Rule 26 on 'Eligibility Code' in 1972 thus providing a great step forward in the formalisation of anti-doping legislation. It was stated that eligible competitors must be amateurs, that they must observe the traditional spirit and ethics of the Games, and that 'the use of drugs or artificial stimulants of any kind is condemned' (Landry and Yerlès 1996: 257). But the results of the tests were hardly convincing. In that year's Games, 2,078 urine samples and 65 blood tests led to seven disqualifications due to positive tests. There were 14 cases of sedatives being used by pentathletes but their international federation disagreed with the view that such substances constituted doping (Landry and Yerlès 1996: 255).

By 1972 a state of some ambivalence pervaded the IOC's anti-doping campaign. On the one hand, de Merode was pushing strongly for more scientific, financial and bureaucratic powers to combat drug abuse. Members would have been aware of the anecdotal evidence of steroid use and seen for themselves the dramatic breaking of records and the changing shape of athletes' bodies. On the other hand, some members were concerned about costs, the science of testing was already some way behind the science of usage, and the problems of definition and imposition were obvious. Moreover, the members from countries where drug taking was rife were not above undermining the efforts of anti-doping experts. Into this fray stepped Lord Killanin to take over from Brundage as President. Killanin was something of a traditionalist himself and deplored the use of drugs. In a 1973 speech he said, 'I believe that doping is a subject as serious as the whole question of eligibility and the size of the games' (cited in Landry and Yerlès 1996: 255). He saw drugs as leading to the creation of artificial men and women. In later writings he expanded on his attitude to drug use. For him the issue was the 'most obnoxious aspect of sport' and that such unfair practices would lead 'to the destruction of competition as we know it' (Killanin 1983: 155). He was suspicious of the Eastern bloc countries where the applications of sports medicine in such a highly regulated manner included the use of steroids, drugs to delay puberty and refining other drugs such as amphetamines. However, he remained sceptical about activities in the USA where the authorities were unwilling to address the problem: there were no drug-testing facilities in the whole country even by the early 1980s. Killanin was a man who had 'lofty ideals', he was dismayed at the speed of modernisation and for him doping was a sign of a much wider malaise:

> The Olympic ideal is to create to the complete person – not an artificial one. Unfortunately, through commercialisation and politicisation, this ideal is being subverted and, through the efforts of certain doctors, the body is being more and more tampered with to its own detriment.
>
> (1983: 161)

As noted in Chapter 5, the Olympics of 1972, Killanin's first in charge, saw a great deal of steroid doping. The arrival of the GDR firmed up scepticism about the activities of some communist countries. However, the IOC does not appear to have supported research into the science of steroid testing, nor had the political differences between countries been addressed. The irony was that de Merode had worked from 1975 towards integrating 'modern biomechanics and its potential advantages for athletes' (Dirix and Sturbois 1998: 27). While he helped push forward the idea of performance enhancement, the doping situation was becoming critical:

> By the time of the 1976 Montreal Olympics steroid usage among Olympic athletes had become not only rampant, but blatant. When observers noted that a number of the East German swim team seemed possessed of several vaguely masculine features, including particularly deep voices, their coach unabashedly replied, 'We have come here to swim, not sing'.
>
> (Laura and White 1991: 6)

However, for all that the IOC Executive was aware of the problem they relied on others to come up with the solutions. Just as Arnold Beckett had worked with researchers in Belgium on a test for amphetamine, so the efforts towards a test for steroids were going on outside of the IOC. When the first tests were introduced in 1976, de Merode's report in the Olympic Review (also presented to a meeting of the International Congress of Olympic Medical Officers) gave no indication of who had funded the research into techniques for testing. However, he did indicate that Raymond Brooks had first discovered the detection method, the radioimmunoassay test. De Merode liked to position the IOC at the forefront of operations, claiming in the report that:

> The analytical testing of the non-medical use of drugs at the Olympic Games in Montreal marked a certain number of steps forward in the long and difficult fight against doping started by the IOC, the International

Federations and other organisations interested in safeguarding the health of athletes and the image of amateur sport.

(de Merode 1979:10)

The results of the tests showed a major discrepancy between anecdotal evidence of doping and the efficacy of the testing system. Of 1800 samples tested for 'traditional doping substances', that is amphetamines, only three proved positive. Of the 275 tested for steroids, eight positives were reported. De Merode assumes this low result can be explained quite easily, 'It is likely that the very small number of positive results is due to the prohibition, later widely publicised, ordered by the [IOC] Medical Commission at its meeting in Innsbruck in 1974' (1979: 16). There is an amazing naïvety, or propaganda, in de Merode's writings. In later years, Ludwig Prokop would mock him in a cartoon that had the Chair of the Medical Commission mouthing the words, 'I expect the Nobel Prize for my fight against doping' (Dirix and Sturbois 1998: 20). De Merode argued that his team were on top of the problem, 'It is very likely that the problem of doping with anabolic steroids will decline in the same way as that of psychomotor stimulants' (1979: 16). And even though he recognised athletes and coaches were constantly working out how to avoid detection or find new drugs, victory would always lie with the side of good. He argued, 'the methods of detection and identification continue to evolve – and this is a recent phenomenon – at a more rapid pace than the discovery and launching of new products. The present period marks perhaps an important step forward from the point of view that the testing possibilities placed at the disposal of sports authorities are no longer outpaced by the attempts to circumvent them' (1979: 16). Like others before him, including Williams, Venerando and Porritt, de Merode expressed profound and mistaken optimism that the doping could be controlled. It is hard to tell if he was knowingly presenting a 'brave face' while being fully aware of the real scope of the issue, or if he did indeed think that science and policy were on top of the problem. It all fitted with the idea that sport was essentially a good thing, populated by and large by people who understood and practiced 'sportsmanship'. As Porritt had explained, in such a paradigm doping was presented as a 'temptation'. None of these prominent scientists and policy advisors admitted (as others had argued) that the myth of sport's ethical purity was just that – a myth. The construction of doping as an evil, a plague, a cancer or a temptation was inspired by this myth, kept alive, and aimed to punish those who failed to live up to its grand expectations. And those who preserved the myth were rewarded for their efforts: La Cava, Williams, Prokop, Venerando, de Merode and Dirix were all awarded the FIMS Gold Medal for contributions to sports medicine. Arthur Gold was given a CBE and knighted for his services to sport.

Yet the reality was different. High performance sports had, by the mid 1970s, become achievement-oriented, technologically innovative, deadly serious, and athletes were obsessive about winning. The hypocrisy was clear. The media, spectators and sports governing bodies wanted great events with heroic athletes breaking records and achieving amazing successes. Yet, they wanted those athletes to know where to stop, to know the difference between healthy and unhealthy aspects of sport, to take some risks but not others, and to sign up for the principles of fair play and sportsmanship. The late 1970s and 1980s would prove to be 'wide open' in terms of doping. The 1950s through to the 1970s set the foundation and the basic principles for anti-doping within which anti-doping has continued to operate and, more to the point, based anti-doping on the myth of pure sport.

Conclusion

The period between 1965 and 1976 was highly influential in the history of doping and anti-doping. It began with Arnold Beckett's improvement and implementation of tests for amphetamine use. European cycling and football were the initial sites of interest for testing, but by 1968 the IOC had introduced it to the Olympics. In America, amphetamine use was widespread but there seems to have been little attempt to seriously tackle it as a problem. Therefore, it was a combination of forces that focused anti-doping in the 1960s. The CoE, FMIS, ANEP, Austrian and French Governments had all made some progress in continental Europe. The BASM had organised a conference, and the IOC had commissioned various scientists to examine the problem. Underlying these were a number of ideologies: amateurism in sport, drugs in society, cultural ethnocentrism and dichotomies of good–evil, pure–corrupt, with the athlete driven by undesired internal and external forces that threatened the sanctity of sport. There was something of a religious crusade to it.

By the early 1970s the problem of steroids was increasingly focusing minds and policies. The science of testing was a more difficult problem to crack. However, researchers in London made the important breakthroughs around 1973–4. A second BASM conference was held in 1975 which spent less time on the philosophy of anti-doping and more on testing. Anti-doping was becoming much more scientific, with research into the effectiveness of steroids increasing, and more complex substances appearing on the market. Yet, both the BASM and the ACSM were guilty of some procrastination as scientists argued about the real value of steroids for improving performance. When the IOC introduced steroid testing in 1976 it caused some optimism that anti-doping could be successful. As we know from the events of the 1980s, such as Ben Johnson's positive test at the 1988 Seoul Olympics and the findings of the Dubin Inquiry (Waddington 2000), steroid use continued almost unhindered by the policies and procedures of anti-doping experts. In more recent years, more funding and research, better international co-operation, and the exposure of the GDR and USSR programmes, have restricted the use of these drugs.

The next chapter will discuss some of the implications of anti-doping and examine the nature of sport itself. A number of writers highlighted in this chapter suggested that drugs were the inevitable outcome of elite sport. In practice, those who promoted anti-doping were closely involved with sport, many were former athletes, and almost all held positions in sports organisations. The arguments against sport lacked power. Anti-doping was an exercise of power in which the

8 Doping, anti-doping and the changing values of sport

Introduction

The historical details presented so far have focused on four broad processes: i) the introduction of drugs into sport in the ambivalent contexts of fatigue reduction and temperance movement pressures; ii) the modernisation of sport and science enhanced by warfare in the period 1920–1945; iii) the growth of amphetamine and steroid usage up to 1976; iv) the emerging ethics and science of anti-doping up to 1976. This narrative has attempted to capture the changes over time in the social construction of knowledge about drugs, acceptance of and resistance to doping, and ethical ideologies of sport. It has been argued that until the late 1950s there was very little stigma attached to drug use in sport, and any anxieties focused on the possible health risks associated with manipulating the central nervous system during a period of sport-induced fatigue. By the early 1960s however history shows a radical about-turn in the official view of doping drugs. In the context of wider social problems associated with drug use, the rapid changes that were occurring in sport, and pressure from a worldwide media trying to find 'scandals', a new discourse of sportsmanship was imposed upon the doping question. Moral dialogues sat uneasily with the ambiguities of science (denial and testing) to set the tone for anti-doping for the rest of the century.

By the mid 1970s two opposing groups faced each other. On one hand, the anti-doping brigade of policy makers, morality-driven pedagogues and scientists; on the other 'cheating' athletes, black market suppliers and scientists inventing new drugs and new ways to beat the testing system. The pseudo-religious underpinning of early anti-doping created a reality of its own: good versus evil. And in the politics of the Cold War the propaganda machine told the public that the communists were all evil, whereas in the West the small minority of wrongdoers did not represent the morality of the people.

There are other fascinating aspects of this history. The pioneers of anti-doping seem to have come from European countries and much of the science was developed in London. Meanwhile, cycling stands out as the sport where drug use was understood as almost part of the sport. The Olympics were the focus for sports purism and idealism, linked directly to the amateur traditions of middle-class track and field. In other words, differences between cultures and between sports underpin this history, suggesting that doping and anti-doping are not based on a universal set of moral codes. Anti-doping was a social construction derived from the ideological, institutional and personal contexts of the day. It was a function of social power, an expression of a 'moral panic' of exaggerated fears and a set of policies with negative unintended consequences. It therefore needs to be critically assessed as an inherently flawed project.

As some contemporary writers observed, however, doping was one symptom of a wider malaise – the problematic modernisation of sport. When sport became a tool of government, a way to make money, a source of status and envy, highly rationalised and bureaucratic, it lost its meaning. This is a central point for any understanding of doping and anti-doping. It does, though, depend on taking up certain positions. What we might call the 'lost innocence' paradigm was based on romantic idealism that sport could unite diverse cultures, could build character, that losing was as noble as winning, and that the competitiveness of elite sport could and should be restrained. More realistically, the rewards – symbolic and economic – that were available especially after the 1950s, meant that sport could never return to the mythical and imagined 'golden age'. To explain doping we need to take a much harder look at what it meant to be involved in top class sport after the Second World War.

The central argument so far is that organisations such as the CoE, BASM and IOC were trying to 'hold the line' of sporting idealism by focusing on the extreme manifestation of unethical behaviour, namely doping. They used modernistic techniques of science, legality and bureaucracy. Yet, paradoxically, they seemed to be fighting against the 'hyper-modernisation' of sport – the use of high-level training techniques, new technologies, and drugs to gain that extra edge. During the 1960s society came to reflect more critically on the nature of modernism. However, that does not fully explain anti-doping. Major sports organisations did not lose their power by allowing the critique to develop, but instead increased their control over athletes and over national systems of sports governance. By the early 1970s the IOC was making formal rules and offering less formal behavioural guidelines that were based on highly Eurocentric cultural values and middle-class paternalistic ideals. Under the guise of 'protection' they could infiltrate almost any country in the world and impose 'global rules'.

National cultures

It would be a mistake to assume that a national culture is responsible for doping or anti-doping. However, aspects of the history presented in the previous seven chapters show that within different countries we can observe specific behaviours, attitudes, institutional responses and outcomes.

The country where most drugs-related activity went on from the 1870s through to the 1970s was the USA. As Bob Goldman argued of the steroids period, some Americans had a can-do mentality, an innate desire for success, and an awareness of the symbolic importance of beating the Soviets. Looking back in history we can see that the examples of Vino-Kolafra, the strung-out six-day cyclists and Thomas Hicks' marathon all show the entrepreneurial spirit of *fin-de-siècle* America being applied to sports. The testimony of some of those involved show a certain optimism that drugs and sport could be married up without being hindered by ethics and health issues. By the interwar period, Americans led the way in exercise physiology, creating the intellectual disciplinary basis for clinical research into drugs for sport. This mirrored increasing demands amongst athletes for any substance or technique to enhance their performance. The Second World War motivated research into amphetamine use even further. Veterans returning from the war and the widespread availability of the drug led to its application to sport from high school up to senior professional sports. By the late 1950s the AMA seemed something of a lone voice trying to stem the tide of amphetamine use. Its concerns did little to prevent drug use continuing. Nor did they trouble John Zeigler when he helped apply the developing science of anabolic steroids for bodybuilders and weightlifters. By the mid 1960s American athletes in a range of sports were using these drugs. The ACSM continued to propagate the 'false dogma' that steroids did not improve performance despite clinical trials and anecdotal evidence to the contrary. Given the lack of testing and the Cold War rivalry, it is hardly surprising that steroid use was rife by the time of the 1976 Olympics.

The British experience has been markedly different. The influence of amateurism and the traditional public school mentality made drugs seem antithetical to sporting competition. Lord Lonsdale's view that using stimulants was 'un-English' typified a middle- and upper-class understanding of what sport was for and what it was all about. Yet, a number of British scientists – not least Sir Robert Christison – had worked on the scientific analysis of stimulants and had used athletic performance situations to test out new drugs. Throughout the interwar period British scientists largely kept their distance from exercise physiology. Athletes did not seem to turn to drugs in their droves, perhaps held back by their amateur ethos. The two prime examples come from professional, working-class football but do offer wonderful stories of experimentation. In the aftermath of the Second World War, the British concern with anti-doping outweighs any evidence of doping practice. Even a decade after the war, when amphetamine use was common in the USA and Europe, British cyclists were naïve innocents thrown into a more professional sporting culture. As William Fotheringham describes Tommy Simpson's arrival on the Continent in 1959:

> In English racing, by and large, drug-taking did not happen. The financial rewards to make it worthwhile were not there; there was no culture of *soigneurs* [coaching assistants] with magic remedies; there was a history of Corinthian amateurism in the sport. All Simpson's English contemporaries speak of seeing drug-taking going on when they arrived in Europe, and being shocked by it.

(2003: 161)

By the late 1950s Adolphe Abrahams was deliberating on the issue, by the early 1960s the BASM had a policy statement, and the key players such as Arthur Porritt, J. G. P. Williams, Martin Lucking, Arnold Beckett and Arthur Gold would take part in early European initiatives towards collective anti-doping. The scientific work that was developed in London and headed by Beckett would result in testing procedures for amphetamines in 1965 and steroids in 1975. This work was supported by major conferences in 1967 and 1975 held under the auspices of the BASM.

It is possible that the British tradition of sport did lend itself towards anti-doping. Corinthian amateurism has played a profound role in the culture and organisation of sport (Allison 2001). Writers on doping in history have drawn attention to the role of 'de-amateurisation' (Waddington 2000). Elsewhere, even very recent contributions to the debate convey a certain regret and a sense of loss:

> If the Corinthian Spirit still survives, however precariously, around the long-off boundary and the Premiership physiotherapy suite, then its spectre still wanders disconsolately here and there through many of the corridors of modern professional life. That it can do is a tribute to the startling resilience of Victorianism and Victorian attitudes a century and more after their official demise. For nothing, it might be said, has suffered more from contemporary notions of 'progress' than amateurism.
>
> (Taylor 2006: 118)

However, such simple explanations are fraught with difficulties. Doping has too long a history to suggest it is only about professionalism. Equally, the critique of amateurism – that it protected the middle-class, male dominance in sport – can be applied to anti-doping. At the same time, anti-doping became a profession in itself with a range of benefits from all-expenses-paid first class travel courtesy of the IOC, to enhanced public profiles for the experts, to attendance at all major sports events. The British attitude seemed to reflect all that was good about amateurism, but in fact offered career opportunism and the extension of social power based on claims of moral superiority.

Germany has had a quite ambivalent history of involvement in doping and anti-doping. Exercise physiology developments in America were mirrored in Germany during the 1920s and 1930s, while use of drugs among German athletes seems to have been commonplace. This history featured heavily in John Hoberman's research (1992, 2005) and he deals in some detail with the continuity (or otherwise) of doping between pre-war Germany and post-war developments in both West and East Germany. However, there has been a wider tendency among writers on doping to imply that both amphetamines and steroids were a product of Nazi science. This fits easily with the 'good versus evil' paradigm and serves to assuage American and European guilt, but it is a simplistic and misleading reading of history. The discontinuity did come however with the creation of East Germany, the state-funded and organised doping regime and the administration of steroid products to females. This does represent the most troubling period in doping history and began in the early 1970s.

The USSR is usually the other 'bogeyman' or 'evil regime' in Western discourses. There is some evidence to support the theory that Soviet athletes, including women, were on steroids from the mid 1950s to 1976. A lot of accusations were made by athletes at that time, and in the late 1980s a flood of empirical information especially from the GDR did prove what most people suspected. So, for example, in 1978 the British thrower Geoff Capes said, 'There is no point in the British athlete competing against a Communist bloc athlete in the field events. He will be beaten by steroids' (cited in Trory 1980: 35). As James Riordan has pointed out, the Soviet Union had a hospitality ship as a medical centre at the 1976 Games to ensure their competitors were 'clean' (1991: 123). Moreover, the post-Glasnost information, particularly that rescued from the Stasi headquarters by Berendonk and Werner shows that the GDR government had put in place a system called State Plan 14.25. As Ivan Waddington broadly noted, 'There is, perhaps, no need to document in detail the multiplicity of ways in which, we now know, members of the sports medicine establishments in the Soviet Union and East Germany were involved in the use of performance-enhancing drugs' (2000: 143). The nature of how this was organised and the complicity of the state troubled Western observers. As Waddington continues, 'What is important to note is that the use of such drugs was a systematic part of Soviet and East German sports policy, and that it involved a wide variety of people, including the "coach-pharmacologist", sports physicians and government ministers' (2000: 143). Given the scale and the exploitative nature of this doping 'regime', the criticisms of these systems do seem valid.

There are a few factors worthy of consideration however that muddy the waters of the 'communists are to blame' theory. First, as Jay Silvester commented in 1972, if nothing else, at least the GDR and USSR had good medical supervision. Second, it is easier to blame others, especially countries that no longer exist, to distract attention from Western culpability. Third, since there were no laws against steroid doping until 1975, it is only from then onwards that these countries can be accused of cheating. Fourth, Western disapproval is enhanced by the role of the state which links directly to criticisms of centralised communist models of government and citizenship. Finally, Western athletes were at least as guilty of doping as their communist counterparts. Arthur Gold commented in 1978 that illegal drug use was much more widespread in British sport than commonly thought and so we should not quickly jump on the bandwagon of accusing the communists (cited in Trory 1980: 35).

Elsewhere in Europe it was professional cycling and football that troubled the authorities. Deaths, sickness, and anecdotal evidence show that amphetamines were widely used in Belgium, France, Italy and Austria. It seems that the circuit of cycling competitions would also involve a travelling pharmacy – what Geoffrey Nicholson (1978) described as an open secret. When the cultures of professional cycling impinged upon the idealised amateur Olympics and resulted in the death of Knud Enemark Jensen, anti-doping got off the ground in the

IOC, BASM and CoE. Therefore, anti-doping policy and science was an amalgam of European concerns about cycling, Olympic and British amateurism and wider pan-national fears of drugs in society. The research on health was ambiguous, so the ideology of sportsmanship was imposed upon the drugs questions. Doping was reinvented as a form of moral deception, a weakness of character, cheating and routinely described from 1963 onwards in pseudo-religious terms as an 'evil'. The Lausanne-based IOC firmed up its anti-doping stance in 1968, and in the columns of the *Bulletin du Comité Internationale Olympique* various international contributors argued against doping. Meanwhile, individual scientists such as Ludwig Prokop and Albert Dirix took anti-doping across boundaries: from the Olympics to professional sports including cycling.

In sum, the ideas relating to drug use and its prohibition varied across international cultures and changed over time within those cultures. The above is not an attempt to outline essentialised cultural traits, but to show that individuals, communities, institutions and broader cultural frames of reference work together to give doping and anti-doping specific meanings.

The ethics and practice of doping in different sports

It has already been argued that the 1960 Rome Olympics bore witness to a clash of cultures. In the broader history of anti-doping and the Olympics however we can also see that certain sports are more problematic than others. In the 1950s and 1960s the power sports such as weightlifting and the throwing events were the ones seen as rife with doping problems. This is because steroids function primarily to build strength and muscle. When the USA and USSR made these sports into literal battles of physical prowess – 'the big arms race' – it was unlikely either side would stop their athletes using steroids. Under the auspices of the IOC however sport was supposed to reflect de Coubertin's romantic idealism, and the explicit use of drugs was not part of that vision. The clash of cultures was again evident. This all served to create a problem of recreational bodybuilding and steroids. Evidence shows a large scale use among amateur athletes, the black market operating through gyms, and dangerous self-experimentation (Monaghan 2001; Waddington 2005).

Cycling offers a fascinating glimpse into changing historical circumstances. During the 1960s a number of riders, famously Jacques Anquetil included, spoke out against drug testing and claimed they had the right to use stimulants. Indeed, anti-doping in cycling was problematic from the beginning. Attempts to impose drug testing or sanctions met with hostility and boycotts, and the UCI saw no feasible way of beating the dopers. Testimony from those involved tells us that, even after the testing improved, cyclists would circumvent the urine test by swapping samples (Voet 2001). In other words, this was the one sport where the participants have, on a wide scale, made it clear they wanted to dope themselves. It is arguably true that the races themselves put so many demands on the competitors that drug use is necessary. Houlihan makes this point when he argues that 'the unrelenting intensity of endurance cycling makes it difficult for athletes to participate without assistance from drugs. In other words, it is the sport which is unnatural rather than the drug-using competitors' (1999: 36).

Most of the other sports where doping emerged were professional. In America, it seems to have been fairly popular in professional football and baseball. One of the features of American sport that made doping more of a public issue was the fact that high school and colleges are much more important and competitive arenas. In European football, by contrast, drugs were sporadically used, but no evidence exists that such a practice disseminated downwards to school or even university level.

As track and field became more professional and nationalistic, doping was more common. Roger Bannister got by experimenting with extra oxygen in the mid 1950s; in the 1960s a few were using amphetamines; by the late 1960s examples of steroid use were beginning to surface. Perhaps the drugs were initially seen as incompatible with track and field, or the sport's historical culture weighed against drug use. Either way, track and field athletes were slower to apply stimulants and steroids to their training and dietary regimes.

Finally, some sports seem to have kept a clean sheet when it comes to doping. Rugby, swimming, cricket, basketball – none of these feature in the pre-1976 period. However, absence of evidence is not the same as evidence of absence. The lack of proper rules and testing means that the opportunity existed to 'cheat'. Many sports organisations wanted to deny their sport might be tainted by drug use rather than work to assess and solve the problem.

A critique of anti-doping

Previous literature has criticised the failings of anti-doping testing and policy in light of evidence of on-going drug use. This is especially pertinent for the period of 1960–1976 when, in spite of strong rhetoric, very little real action was taken. However, this section presents three alternative forms of critique. First, that anti-doping was really about the exercise of power. Second, that it was an overreaction and a 'moral panic' whose underlying 'problem' was less convincing. Third, that policies had a range of negative unintended consequences.

When anti-doping was first emerging in the late 1950s it was evident that it was an authoritarian discourse advanced by elite groups in society. By the mid 1960s these factors were still in place but a further dimension of practical control had been introduced. Rules, tests and punishments would be the technologies of power. The subjects of this disciplinary regime – or anti-doping 'gaze' – were forced to agree to these procedures or risk losing their livelihood. Testing was a genuine infringement of personal space from the beginning: the sex tests on women were the worst case, but having a stranger observe the passing of urine is humiliating. Worse still, everyone was a suspect and had to prove their innocence by passing a series of tests set by the authorities. Even if they did pass, athletes who performed especially well in an event would be under suspicion of doping by the authorities and their rivals. Once it became clear that tests were fallible, almost every athlete became a potential cheat. If doping threatened the very nature of sport by the early 1970s it was not just because of drug use, but the processes by which cheating was defined, suspected and not adequately resolved. The air of suspicion was created by those in power who constructed the 'witch-hunt'.

Power rested with elite groups, especially with middle- and upper-class individuals who had previously been athletes, then went on to prestigious careers in medicine or sports administration. They wanted to fashion sport in their image: the established amateur traditional culture. The Chairman of the IOC's Medical Commission was a prince, almost every anti-doping scientist was a doctor or professor, Arthur Porritt was eventually knighted, given a peerage and made Governor-General of New Zealand. These examples show how elitist anti-doping was from the beginning. Like the Victorian rational recreationists (Holt 1992) they saw sport in idealistic terms, capable of improving the character and lifestyles of those who might descend into anarchy and degeneration. Many anti-doping experts had been former athletes: Porritt competed in the 1924 Olympics while a medical student at Oxford University then was the New Zealand team manager at the 1934 Empire Games and the 1936 Berlin Olympics. Martin Lucking was an Olympic shot-putter in the 1960s. Men who grew up being inculcated into the values of sport wanted to pass that on to the next generation.

The targets for anti-doping were those who misused sport, who ruined its noble aims: professionals, communists, working classes, and any others who didn't sign up to the middle-class morality of sport. The imbalance of power and social status is striking. Athletes were not invited to policy discussions or conferences such as those held by the CoE or BASM. When they chose to speak out against anti-doping or refused to take tests they were condemned in the media and punished by their sport's authority. Anti-doping was imposed from above without consultation, dialogue or empathy – it is no wonder many athletes put so much energy into trying to cheat the system. This was an 'us versus them' oppositional divide from the beginning.

The second critique about anti-doping is that it was a 'moral panic' that exaggerated the consequences of drug use in terms of both health effects and fair play. It is curious that the shift in social attitudes to amphetamines happened so quickly. In the 1940s and 1950s they were a panacea for all manner of ailments, by the 1960s they were a social tragedy. Yet, the extent of usage and the lack of clear evidence suggest the health problems associated with the drug were not all that serious. Even the cases of fatalities and serious accidents could have been explained by a range of factors including exhaustion, dehydration, overheating, lack of medical supervision, and the demands of the sport. Instead, it was drugs alone that were blamed. The testing of cycling and football that occurred in Italy and Belgium around this time showed fairly high levels of usage without any serious illnesses or deaths. The lack of medical cases of drug-related problems among American athletes between the 1950s and 1970s shows that usage could be widespread without any dire consequences. Poor judgement, addiction and hospitalisation may occur in rare examples such as that of Everton goalkeeper Albert Dunlop, but he was a heavy user and an alcoholic. The sorts of doses Mandell admitted giving American football players caused little more than extra aggressiveness. Even the anti-doping expert Max Novich (1964) recognised that the addictive effects of amphetamines for athletes had been exaggerated. And at the BASM conference on steroids in 1975, A. H. Payne told the audience that 'it is common knowledge that the dire warnings of the health hazards have been overrated. I know of one athlete who has been on steroids almost non-stop for nine years and he is a fit healthy bull, who enjoys his sex life. There are side effects, but these appear to be only minor' (1975: 87). But the argument of ath-lete choice was given short shrift: it was simply assumed that elite competitors could not be trusted to manage the risk appropriately. Even minor doses were made illegal and the all-encompassing legal framework set in motion.

At the same time, the argument that doping betrayed the principles of fair play was also overplayed. There are any number of ways in which sport is not a level playing field: from genetic inheritance to access to resources to psychological assistance and good coaching. In fact, the point of training and preparation is to make the playing field uneven. So the attempt to connect sportsmanship with some notion of purity and positive life force led to the oppositional idea that drugs, cheating and corruption went hand-in-hand and would result in the death of sport. Yet, as some of the pre-war writers on doping illustrated, the boundaries between stimulant drugs and other forms of enhancement were extremely blurred (Bøje 1939). When does a natural substance such as oxygen, altitude or even testosterone become cheating? How is taking a chemical substance that much dif-ferent from using specialised equipment, psychological counselling or team tactics? The notion that sport was about matching individuals' natural talents was already an anachronism. Modern sport was about using the available techniques to one's best advantage, not about imagining days gone by when sport existed purely for enjoyable recreation, fitness and character building. More to the point, this was a myth anyway that gets reinvented whenever powerful social groups wish to assert their values and establish greater control over troublesome subjects.

Finally in this section there is the question of unintended consequences. Anti-doping created a new universe for sport, one in which the athlete was the focus of a range of technical, legal and moral strategies. They were placed under constant supervision, scrutiny and assumed to be opportunists who would break the rules if given the scope to do so. Doping was a very serious business. Those who missed tests or dropped out of competitions where testing was to take place, were immediately assumed guilty. When a group of successful athletes appeared from a specific country, especially 'closed' communist countries, it was assumed they were on drugs. The world of sport had become tainted forever with accusa-tions, scandal, guilt and the great witch-hunt. Yes, the greed and obsession of athletes who used drugs was partly to blame, but the overarching demands of anti-doping also contribute to this unfolding drama. In other words, the dis-courses of doping were not about the drugs themselves but about the ways in which anti-doping campaigners reconstructed their social meanings.

More pragmatically, testing led athletes to experiment with new drugs whose health effects and safe dosage levels were unknown. It led them to risky 'masking' techniques using substances such as diuretics or to load up on steroids and rapidly come off them a few weeks before an event. It led to the search for undetectable methods such as blood doping where blood is removed, stored and re-injected to boost red cell counts after training. All this messing about with hormonal levels and blood must have been at least as unhealthy as the taking of amphetamines and steroids were in the first place.

By the late 1970s a similar critique was developing about Western health care in general. The points raised by John Ehrenreich in his 1978 anthology which develops what he calls a 'cultural critique' of medicine in society, show parallels with the above assessment of anti-doping during this period. He distances himself from the 'political economy critique' which assumes the provision of health services per se to be admirable but searches for better ways of distributing and managing healthcare (much like the anti-doping policy discussions that assume the principles to be sound but the administration to be less than perfect):

> Modern medical care, contrary to the assumptions of the more traditionally radical political economy critique, does not consist of the administration by doctors of a group of morally neutral, essentially benign and effective techniques for curing disease and reducing pain and suffering. The techniques themselves are frequently useless and all too often actually physically harmful. The 'scientific' knowledge of the doctors is sometimes not knowledge at all, but rather social messages (e.g., about the proper behaviour of women) wrapped up in technical language. And above all, both the doctor–patient relationship and the entire structure of medical services are not mere technical relationships, but social relationships which express and reinforce (often in subtle ways) the social relations of the larger society: e.g., class, racial, sexual and age hierarchy; individual isolation and passivity; and dependency on the social order itself in the resolution of both individual and social problems.
>
> (1978: 15)

A critique of elite sport

The early discourses on anti-doping, from the mid 1950s onwards, can be interpreted in a number of ways. They may be an overinflated attempt to moralise and establish control over sport and over deviant sections of society. They may be a projection on to sport of middle-class anxieties about drug misuse, sexual profligacy, political radicalism, and cultural decadence. They may represent a clash of cultures between generations: the pre-war sober, austere, amateurs up against the progressive nationalistic, professional and scientifically inclined post-war innovators. These are interconnected and each a partial explanation. However, just as interesting was the manner in which sport itself came under discussion around that period in a way that rarely occurred from the 1970s onwards. The ideology underlying elite competitive sport is now a consensus, and any one who challenges it will probably be dismissed as a neo-Marxist, wishy-washy liberal, or jealous failed athlete.

There are two questions here. First, was doping the consequence of elite sport itself? Second, was anti-doping a genuine response to changes in sport that began in the early post-war period and were enhanced in the 1960s?

The reasons why athletes turn to drugs is because they are driven by internal and external pressures that supersede any sense that sport should be enjoyably competitive and socially valuable. In 1953 E. McDonald Bailey, the Trinidadian sprinter who competed for England, offered his view on sportsmanship, 'I do not advocate a win-at-all-costs approach. Always keep inside the rules of the game and the accepted ethics of moral conduct' (1953: 100). That did not mean giving up easily or not enjoying the thrill of victory, but that a line should be drawn before the athlete resorts to cheating. Of course, it could easily be argued that since drug use was not banned during the 1950s there was nothing in this definition of sportsmanship to prevent someone taking amphetamines, strychnine, cocaine or any other such drug. Bailey made reference to the controversy over Douglas Jardine's captaincy of the England cricket team that went to Australia to employ the 'bodyline' bowling technique that targeted the batsman's body. He sees this as acceptable as victory was the principle objective and the methods used were within the laws of the game. It might be argued that the backlash against Jardine was simply the traditionalists' retort to a moderniser.

So doping cannot simply be seen as a transgression of sportsmanship when that could include 'borderline' legal strategies. Nor can doping be simply connected to professionalism. The desire to boost performance can be seen throughout the twentieth century. The other external pressure was national prestige, but it was more club level success than national prestige that inspired football managers to give drugs to their players. And it was individual success that motivated cyclists and many track and field athletes.

Perhaps the real flaw in these sorts of explanations is that they construct doping as a problem. Even theories which point to personal obsession, insecurities, anxieties, fear of failure, and all-consuming will to win, suggest something is fundamentally wrong with the soul of the athlete. However, writers on wider drug use in society have argued that governmental and other authoritarian discourses from the eighteenth century onwards deny the essential 'pleasure' inherent in drug use:

> A number of quite diverse official discourses across a long time span, from the 'beastliness' of 18th century vice to 'social determination' of modernist criminology, turn out to have one feature in common: problematic activities are managed and discussed in ways that deny or silence the voluntary and reasonable seeking of enjoyment as warrantable motives. Governmental discourses about drugs and alcohol, in particular, tend to remain silent about pleasure as a motive for consumption, and raise instead visions of a consumption characterized by compulsion, pain and pathology. Problematic substance use is said to be caused not by pleasure-seeking but by such things as the 'slavery of the will' characteristic of alcoholics; by the 'behavioural

stimuli' of many current psychological theories of 'craving'; or by some other bodily, social or psychological failing or deficit that pushes people to act 'unreasonably'.

(O'Malley and Valverde 2004: 26)

The tendency to argue that doped athletes are irrational obsessives who have lost control of their minds and are willing to punish their bodies distracts us from the possibility that some athletes might choose to dope, that they might take pleasure in it, and might have perfectly rationalised logical reasons for doing so. The pleasure comes from winning so the logic behind doping is actually the logic of sport itself. When critics try to impose a framework of risk they are effectively missing the point. A joyless life of losing is nothing to an athlete who seeks the pleasures of success. This is not about money or social status or bringing prestige to a local or national community. As Verner Møller has argued, athletes 'participate because they are attracted to the competition. The contest is the motivation' (2003: 16). This is about sport, about winning: the desire that drives an athlete to train and compete is precisely the same desire that leads them to dope. Trying to draw a line between the two is, for many, abstract and pointless.

Which brings us to the second question, was anti-doping a response to changes in sport? Those working inside sport must have realised that drugs were increasingly a part of the scene in a number of places. Drugs created a type of unfairness, a boost that had not been earned by training or by developing skill techniques. Once a number of competitors used them, they all had to, if the pleasures of success and the logic of the will to win remained motivating factors. In 1960, Tommy Simpson told a journalist, 'I am up there with the stars, but then suddenly they will go away from me. I know from the way they ride the next day that they are taking dope. I don't want to have to take it – I have too much respect for my body – but if I don't win a big event soon, I shall have to start taking it' (cited in Fotheringham 2003: 148).

Early anti-doping pioneers did not like the drugs that were being used which had a poor reputation in society that reflected badly on sport. They did not like the extent of drug use that would lead eventually to all athletes feeling obliged to use them. They also thought success had to be fought for, not handed out on a plate, drunk from a bottle or injected. However, sport was showing other signs of excess: political tensions in the Cold War rivalry; conspicuous alcoholism and sexual promiscuity among players; and an erosion of the ideals of playing the game and gentlemanly conduct. The hopeful motto of the traditional pedagogues, 'it's not the winning but the taking part that counts', was a joke.

If the problem of doping lies in the logic of sport it worsened through the post-war decades as training methods began to take over athletes' lives. Such were the increased standards of competition that in order to achieve anything at international level, potentially talented athletes had to be identified and developed at the earliest opportunity and then had to dedicate themselves to their sport. When children as young as six or seven years old are streamlined into sports, perhaps even taken out of normal schools to attend specialist sports academies, clearly the desire to produce winning athletes has gone too far. Even if the training regimes are not imposed until later in life, athletes can become institutionalised, have a narrow set of skills, and little contact with the outside world. They sacrifice the usual rites of passage of teenage years in favour of their sporting career. Moreover, their bodies are delicate machines that operate at the optimal level of performance, having been worked upon by coaches, nutritionists and scientists for several years. If elite sport produces the obsessed, focused, asocial types who eventually take drugs as one more element in their preparation for events, then the critical focus must widen. Doping may simply be a convenient scapegoat that draws attention from the heart of the matter – the logic and structure of sport itself.

James Riordan's writings on the Soviet Union are far more critical of the overall problems of systematic, almost ruthless, talent identification than of the doping which was simply one more symptom of a deeper malaise. The GDR focused on sports as a means of displaying nationality on the world stage, and the institutionalisation of sports medicine and talent development happened in parallel with doping. The high social status given to successful athletes in America from high school upwards means that finding that extra edge for victory would have a longer-term benefit for individuals.

It was the demands of long events and over 200 days a year of racing that many cyclists used to justify their use of drugs. In 1967 the top Belgian rider Rik Van Steenbergen wrote in a newspaper article:

> I've had to drive to Paris, then immediately after the race get back in my car for a 10-hour trip to Stuttgart where I had to get on my bike at once. There was nothing to do. An organiser would want this star or that one on the bill. He would pay for it. Another would want the same ones the next day, and the public wanted something for its money. As a result, the stars had to look fresh in every race, and they couldn't do that without stimulants. There are no supermen. Doping is necessary in cycling.
>
> (cited in Fotheringham 2003: 166)

For all that Pierre Dumas, Albert Dirix and Ludwig Prokop worried about the amounts and types of drugs cyclists were using, none of them spoke up to say the conditions under which cyclists operated were fundamentally to blame. It was easier to focus on sportsmanship, individual behaviour, and constructing methods of detection. The same can be said for Olympic anti-doping. The problem was never related to the frenzy and hype over the quadrennial event itself but to the fringe minority of cheats who had poor ethical principles and needed to be rooted out through efficient testing procedures. The fact that anti-doping was led by the IOC means that critical reflection on Olympic sports culture and processes was never going to happen. Instead, the metaphors used suggested a healthy 'body' which was being attacked from the outside by 'disease'. As Arnold Beckett put it, 'deaths in sport were necessary before leaders and legislators were shaken out of their complacency and mobilized a counterattack upon the cancer which had been established in the body of sport and was becoming increasingly invasive' (1988: 655).

Yet sport is fundamentally about winning, hierarchy, elitism and losers get nothing. It encourages people to think of others as enemies. Bias and partisanship are actively promoted. It demarcates the best from the rest, it is all about physical and social superiority. It is a harsh system that is not just intolerant towards failure but explicitly rejects those who fail. It favours the economically developed countries who can provide their athletes with the best resources and who can 'cherry-pick' talent from underdeveloped countries. Meanwhile, the futile use of money in professional sport stands as a tragic waste when so much of the world remains poverty-stricken. In other words, sport needed to be critically assessed – the 'panic' over doping was a smokescreen.

Conclusion

This book set out to explain the emergence and growth of doping, and the regulatory response known as anti-doping. This has proved to be something of a complicated history to overview and summarise because so much of it depends on a quite subjective view of what sport has been and should be about.

It has been argued that doping formed part of the culture of sport since the late nineteenth century. The international development of sports science and medicine in the interwar period provided new knowledge, ideas and substances for enhancing performance. This period shows two things: that sport never had a 'golden age', but that drugs were not always seen as 'evil'. Most scientists and writers assumed that if a substance did not damage the health of the athlete it was morally acceptable.

The second major element of the story is the connection of research into stimulants with the military objectives of the Second World War. This loosened the grip of health ethics and allowed researchers a wider scope of experimental design. The race between the Allies and Germans to develop amphetamine drugs for soldiers and pilots, combined with the perceived effectiveness of these drugs, meant that such stimulants had a positive aura in the immediate post-war period.

It was not long however before the backlash began. European scientists were concerned about the overuse of drugs by cyclists while other health experts linked drugs in sport to wider social drugs issues. Indeed, the moral panic over drugs in society was sharpened in the late 1950s and into the 1960s, providing a parallel context for the development of anti-doping in sport. Some commentators at the time explicitly linked the two processes. The other movement was a panic over the changing nature of sport: it was becoming too nationalistic, professional and serious for the tastes of those brought up in pre-war amateurism. What this really posed was a threat to the patriarchal, middle-class dominance of sports culture and sporting organisations. There was also a latent anxiety over the changing nature of female bodies that also threatened this power structure.

By the late 1960s and into the 1970s, anti-doping experts had created a modernistic system of surveillance methods, bureaucratic machinery, and legal powers that changed the face of sport. All athletes were potential cheats, and even the slightest deviance from the written rules could lead to public shame and a lengthy ban from sport. However, there was a profound paradox that was never properly resolved and which remains the central point of crisis in anti-doping to this day. Was sport pure in essence but corrupted by 'cancers' such as doping linked to other problems such as professionalism? Or was sport actually about winning and doing whatever it takes to be a champion?

This book has offered a critique of anti-doping that has led to a critique of sport. The central argument has been that anti-doping did not offer a realistic vision of modern sport. Even by the 1960s, fantasies of sportsmanship, amateurism and peaceful co-operation through sport were anachronistic at best, delusional at worst. The result was a system of drug testing and punishment out of kilter with the demands of high performance sport; a system that is better understood as a consequence of various social elements than as a simple, politically neutral, response to a problem everyone could agree upon. Finally, perhaps the most interesting voices were those of Milton Roemer, Herbert Berger, M. Hollyhock and Georg van Opel who tried in vain to suggest that sport itself was the problem. They were the true heroes, fighting the lonely battle, knowing full well that sport was waist-high in hypocrisy. It is their legacy that should be revived – the honest appraisal of elite sport in the modern world.

Epilogue

In 1999 the IOC conceded some ground and accepted that anti-doping needed an autonomous controlling authority, and so the World Anti-Doping Agency was established. Prince Alexandre de Merode and the Medical Commission he chaired had led the fight against doping for 32 years. The arguments for WADA were convincing: the problem had grown so much that sports authorities that had other responsibilities could not police drug use on an international scale. By 2006, WADA had developed a full remit of scientific and educational projects with priority areas including the development of a test for human growth hormone. But a certain pessimism dominates the doping debate as anti-doping enthusiasts cannot see how the threat of genetic manipulation can be stopped.

The apparent impossibility of detecting gene therapy as a form of enhancement has been presented as a significant rationale for liberalising doping. For Andy Miah, this point is more convincing than the arguments made against anti-doping in the 1990s (Miah 2004). And yet, it is very unlikely WADA or any national sports authority would allow or encourage genetic changes for the sake of sporting success: if nothing else the adverse publicity would deter them.

Does history help with the liberalisation debate? This book has shown that doping has been integral to sport – even if only episodic during certain time periods – since the 1870s. It has also shown that as sport (and society) went through a process of modernisation, so drugs became available as a by-product of the rational, technological and scientific approach to the human body as a machine of performance. The great nineteenth-century image of the human motor may have receded from popular culture and from industry, but it remains central to high performance sport. Following that line, it could be argued that turning the body into a machine represents the dehumanisation of the athlete and thus the elite level athlete exists in a world that should not be restricted by such traditional moralities as fair play or even good health. Sport is not about a level playing field – it is about the exact opposite, trying to make the playing field unlevel. Athletes know what they want, they know the risks, there are other risks that are accepted, drugs are only one more technological enhancement. So let them do it. And, as Ben Johnson has argued, all spectators want is the spectacle: the fastest man or woman on the planet, the highest jumper, the longest thrower. They don't care how that individual got to be so good at their chosen pursuit.

History tells us that athletes are people who are driven to their obsessive goals by an irrational will to win. It also tells us that the broader structure of economic and nationalist rewards motivates doctors and athletes to cheat. The lesson of detailing anti-doping from the late 1950s is that doping was constructed as a fringe problem brought into sport by those whose 'evil' desires warped something that was essentially 'good'. This was a moral judgement based on a very specific imagery of sport and society. The question is whether we wish to see doping as the product of political and commercial forces that used available science, or if we wish to see doping as the inevitable outcome of the logic of sport that actually drove scientific innovations.

Instead, as Møller has shown quite convincingly:

> The idea that sport is ennobling is, it would seem, false. On the contrary, it seems reasonable to argue in favour of the opposite: sport contains the seeds of violence and moral decay. The idea that sport is fundamentally a good thing derives from the fact that, rooted in the traditional folk games, it was adapted and civilised by the leisure class and thereby connected to the ideal of the gentleman.
>
> (2003: 16)

Given that the idealism surrounding sport can be deconstructed, Møller goes further to argue that doping is an outcome of the logic of sport and indeed of the logic of modernity. John Hoberman has countered this by asserting the value of Møller's attempts to place doping in social and economic context, but notes, 'I do not share his view that the right to practice doping is an inherent part of elite sport' (2003: 126). This does not answer the question though of how to provide an adequate rationale for anti-doping if we accept that a) sports idealism is flawed; b) sport is a medicalised, technologised process which cares little for fantasies for fair play and a level playing field; and c) health risks persist throughout sport and athletes ought to be allowed to judge for themselves which risks they are allowed to take.

To bring this back to the contemporary debate, it could easily be argued that modern sport has come so far that it would be impossible to persuade athletes to resist doping or other illegal enhancements. There has been, ever since the mid 1960s, a ridiculous game of cat and mouse going on in which one move by the authorities prompted another by the users (Reiterer 2000). Doping and anti-doping are in a double-bind: one cannot exist without the other, they feed off each other; action leads to reaction leads to reaction. Each side requires more specialists and more funding – effectively the principle outcome is power.

When approached from this more radical perspective, sport can be represented as a meaningless activity around which has been built structures of professionalism and resources that provide careers and profits. The doping/anti-doping nexus produces experts who gain prestige and careers, either as 'underground' doping innovators or as the public faces of anti-doping policy.

The whole anti-doping mythology placed a great deal of pressure on those working in sports policy who were genuinely concerned with the classic twin concerns of fair play and health. They had to make quick decisions to control what was seen as an emerging problem. They had to respond to structural circumstances: media presentation, athletes' expectation, and the power struggles of policy makers and sports authorities. They had genuine concerns that liberalisation would seriously impact on competitors' health and on the nature of sport. However, the paradoxical nature of sport in modern culture ties people to certain discourses. Fair play and health are elements of this discourse which were empowered by the events of the early 1960s. Yet, performance sport does not put either of these elements into practice. Facing up to this paradox, to the continuing conflict of the amateur idealism set against modern performance science, seems almost impossible. Especially when the alleged outcome will be a hypermodernist nightmare of robot athletes and genetic freaks.

So what we need is a new vision of sport. We have to accept that sport is a technological process – the taking of a physical body and making it into something new in pursuit of athletic achievement. We also have to accept that the logic of the will to win drives athletes to search out any innovation that will help their cause. Sometimes they need to be protected from themselves, like the anorexic or the obsessive-compulsive. Yet, it is impossible to hide from the critique of sport, that the rewards and internalisation processes can lead to severe psychological and emotional imbalances. Sport itself can be a bad influence. Drugs are part of that problem. If we can manage the excesses of sport then we might be able to manage the doping problem. This is not part of the current debate though. Certainly, in the UK the principal sports issue is how to develop more talented elite level athletes for winning medals at the London Olympics in 2012. As it stands, modern societies seem to want more sport, not less. They seem obsessed with the idea of successful achievement, and very few voices of dissent are heard which suggest sport is a pointless distraction from the important things in life.

If we want sport, we cannot have it both ways. We cannot have great moments of physical transcendence, of pushing forward the boundaries of human perfection, of idealising the athletic body, and have clean, pure, upright competitors. Sport is destructive when it demands that athletes lose all sense of perspective in their pursuit of glory. But in life, in art, in music, in science, in philosophy, it is always those who lose their sense of perspective that make a lasting impact on the world. Jimi Hendrix died young but left amazing, inspiring music. Albert Einstein was unconventional and eccentric, but a genius. Zinedane Zidane made football into an art form but had moments of madness. Why do we expect athletes to conform and be brilliant at the same time?

Similarly, why do we expect athletes to be perfect role models? So many other prominent people are allowed their lapses into drugs, alcohol and other vices. We do not stop rock stars, supermodels and media executives from doing their jobs when they are caught taking drugs. And we do not expect young people to stop listening to rock music or watching TV because of the drug use in these industries.

Is it possible to have a new set of ethics once we accept that sport has been changed by science and the cult of victory? As Vernon Howard wrote, we can no longer draw our ethics from the past:

In the back of my mind as I began to write this essay [on anti-doping] was something like the atmosphere of *Chariots of Fire*, an atmosphere not unlike my own competitive days [in the 1950s and 1960s]. Sadly, as I ruminated further on the complexities of fair play and doping in sport, I realised that the relatively simple conditions of the past no longer existed. My knee-jerk responses were obsolete. That fact, however, gradually became a challenge to me; a challenge to re-articulate what it is to be a fair and honest competitor in an age of biochemical technology.

(1991: 56–7)

He realised this was far from simple, 'If I have done no more than raise certain perplexities to the level of philosophical examination, I am satisfied' (1991: 57).

I would argue that it is less tragic that the simple conditions of the past are gone, than that athletes are still being punished for their failure to respect traditional values in a modern age. Rather than search for meaning in the myths and fantasies of bygone eras, modern debates on drugs and other forms of performance enhancement should confront the reality that ethics have changed and that sport has changed.

Notes

1 Sport, drugs and society

1 The word athlete will be used as a generic term for a competitor in any sports event, not just for track and field. This is preferred to the gender-specific 'sportsman' or the convoluted 'sportsman or -woman' or the plain ugly 'sportsperson'.

4 Amphetamines and post-war sport, 1945–1976

1 Further research is required on Eastern European countries in this respect.

5 The steroids epidemic, 1945–1976

1 Such progress tapered off, possibly as the limits were being reached even with steroids, so that by 1986 the record was 86.74m and held by the Soviet thrower Yuriy Sedykh. Perhaps more telling however is the fact that this record has never been surpassed. Even by the 2004 Olympics the longest throw was 83.19m by Adrian Annus of Hungary – who then was stripped of the title for failing to turn up for a second test after the officials suspected that he faked his urine test the first time.
2 This John Williams is probably the same person cited in earlier chapters as J. G. P. Williams.

6 Dealing with the scandal: Anti-doping and the new ethics of sport, 1945–1965

1 Beta-phenyl-isopropylamine is a type of methamphetamine.
2 MAO stands for mono-amine-oxidase which is a class of drug used to treat depression, i.e. that would have a stimulant effect.
3 Even by 1991, Arnold Beckett assumed Prokop's version of Jensen's death to be true. He wrote, 'Attention focused on this problem in 1960 at the Olympic Games in Rome when three Danish cyclists were taken to hospital and one, Jensen, died. His death was associated with the use of stimulant drugs' (Beckett 1991: 26).

References

Abrahams, A. (1958) 'The Use and Abuse of Drugs by Athletes', *British Journal of Addiction*, 55 (1): 23–7.

Alles, G. A. and Feigen, G. A. (1942) 'The Influence of Benzedrine on Work Decrement and Patellar Reflex', *American Journal of Physiology*, 136: 392.

Allison, L. (2001) *Amateurism in Sport: An Analysis and a Defence*, London, Frank Cass.

Andrews, G. and Solomon, D. (1975) 'Coca and Cocaine: Uses and Abuses' in Andrews, G. and Solomon, D. (eds) *The Coca Leaf and Cocaine Papers*, New York and London, Harcourt Brace Jovanovich.

Andrews, M. (undated) 'Written by J. Maxwell Andrews' in the Harold Abrahams Collection, University of Birmingham Library, NCAL XXV H27.

Anstie, F. E. (1864) *Stimulants and Narcotics, Their Mutual Relations: With Special Researches on the Action of Alcohol, Aether and Chloroform*, London, Macmillan & Co.

BASM (1969) 'Statement on Doping', *British Journal of Sports Medicine*, 4 (2): 109–10

BASM (1975a) 'Editorial', *British Journal of Sports Medicine*, 9 (2): 58–9.

BASM (1975b) 'Summaries', *British Journal of Sports Medicine*, 9 (2): 110.

BBC (2005a) *Timeshift: Drugs in Sport*, 15 June, BBC2.

BBC (2005b) *Reputations: Ben Johnson*, 15 June, BBC2.

Beamish, R. and Ritchie, I. (2004) 'From Chivalrous "Brothers-in-Arms" to the Eligible Athlete: Changed Principles and the IOC's Banned Substance List', *International Review for the Sociology of Sport*, 39 (4): 355–71.

Beamish, R. and Ritchie, I. (2005) 'From Fixed Capacities to Performance-Enhancement: The Paradigm Shift in the Science of "Training" and the Use of Performance-Enhancing Substances', *Sport in History*, 25 (3): 412–33.

Beckett, A. (1976) 'Problems of Anabolic Steroids in Sport', *Olympic Review*, Nov–Dec, no. 109–10: 591–8.

Beckett, A. (1986) 'Philosophy and Practice of Control of Drug Abuse in Sport, Part I', in Gorrod, J. W., Gibson, G. G. and Mitchard, M. (eds) *Development of Drugs and Modern Medicines: A Conference to Honour Professor Arnold H. Beckett*, Chichester, Ellis Horwood.

Beckett, A. (1988) 'The doping problem', in Dirix, A., Knuttgen, H. G. and Tittel, K. (eds) *The Olympic Book of Sports Medicine: Volume 1 of the Encyclopaedia of Sports Medicine*, Oxford, Blackwell.

Beckett, A. (1991) 'The future of the Olympic movement', in Laura, R. S. and White, S. W. (eds) *Drug Controversy in Sport: The Socio-Ethical and Medical Issues*, Sydney, Allen & Unwin.

Beckett, A. H., Tucker, G. T. and James, R. D. (1966) *Bulletin of the British Association of Sports Medicine*, 2: 113–27.

Bennett, A. H. (1873) 'An Experimental Inquiry into the Physiological Actions of Theine, Guaranine, Cocaine and Theobromine', *Edinburgh Medical Journal*, 19: 323–41.

Bennett, A. H. (1874) 'The Physiological Action of Coca', *British Medical Journal*, 1: 510.

Berridge, V. (1999) *Opium and the People: Opiate Use and Drug Control Policy in Nineteenth and Early Twentieth Century England*, London and New York, Free Association Books.

Bøje, O. (1939) 'Doping: A Study of the Means Employed to Raise the Level of Performance in Sport', *Bulletin of the Health Organisation of the League of Nations*, 8: 439–68.

Booth, D. (2005) *The Field: Truth and Fiction in Sports History*, London, Routledge.

Bowler, P. J. and Morus, I. R. (2005) *Making Modern Science: A Historical Survey*, Chicago and London, University of Chicago Press.

British Medical Journal (1967) Editorial, 4: 310.

Brooks, R. V., Firth, R. G. and Sumner, D. A. (1975) 'Detection of Anabolic Steroids by Radioimmunoassay', *British Journal of Sports Medicine*, 9: 89–92.

Browne, R. C. (1947) 'Amphetamine in the Air Force', *British Journal of Addiction*, 44 (2): 64–70.

Budd, M. A. (1997) *The Sculpture Machine: Physical Culture and Body Politics in the Age of Empire*, New York, New York University Press.

Bulletin du Comité International Olympique (1954) 'Is the Oxygenation of Athletes a Form of Doping?' April, 45: 24–5.

Bulletin du Comité International Olympique (1955) 'Quotation of Outside Opinion', November, 52: 54.

Bulletin du Comité International Olympique (1961) 'News in Brief', November, 76: 30.

Bulletin du Comité International Olympique (1962a) 'In Switzerland, the National Physical Education Association is Waging War Against the Practice of Doping', May, 78: 53–4.

Bulletin du Comité Internationale Olympique (1962b) 'Waging War Against Dope', February, 77: 46.

Christensen, E. H. (1931) 'Beiträge zur Physiologie schwerer körperlicher Arbeit', *Arbeitsphysiologie*, 4: 453.

Christison, R. (1876) 'Observations on the Effects of Cuca, or Coca, the Leaves of Erythroxylon Coca', *British Medical Journal*, April 29, 527–31.

Collins, T. and Vamplew, W. (2002) *Mud, Sweat and Beers: A Cultural History of Sport and Alcohol*, Oxford, Berg.

CoE (1964) *Council of Europe Committee for Out-of-School Education, Doping of Athletes: Reports of the Special Working Parties*, Strasbourg, Council of Europe.

CoE (1989) *Anti-Doping Convention, Explanatory Note Appendix*, Strasbourg, Council of Europe.

Courtwright, D. T. (1995) 'The Rise and Fall and Rise of Cocaine in the United States', in Goodman, J., Lovejoy, P.E. and Sherratt, A., *Consuming Habits: Drugs in History and Anthropology*, London and New York, Routledge.

Courtwright, D. T. (2001) *Forces of Habit: Drugs and the Making of the Modern World*, Cambridge, Mass. and London, Harvard University Press.

Crichton-Miller, H. (1947) 'Subjective and Objective Observations on Benzedrine', *British Journal of Addiction*, 44 (2): 46–9.

Crump, J. (1966) *Running Round the World*, London, Hale.

Cuthbertson, D. P. and Knox, J. A. C. (1947) 'The Effects of Analeptics on the Fatigued Subject', *Journal of Physiology*, 106: 42–58.

Daily Herald , 14 September 1964.

Daily Mail, 10 September 1962.

de Coubertin, P. (1894) 'Speech at the Closing Banquet of the Congress of Paris', reprinted in Müller, N. (ed) (2000) *Pierre de Coubertin, 1863–1937. Olympism: selected writings*, Lausanne: IOC, 531–2.

de Kruif, P. (1945) *The Male Hormone: A New Gleam of Hope for Prolonging Man's Prime of Life*, New York, Harcourt, Brace & Co.

de Merode, A. (1979) 'Doping Tests at the Olympic Games in 1976', *Olympic Review*, January, 135: 10–16.

de Merode, A. (1999) 'Introduction and Background', *Doping: An IOC White Paper*, Lausanne, IOC.

Denham, B. (1999) 'On Drugs in Sports in the Aftermath of Flo-Jo's Death, Big Mac's Attack', *Journal of Sport and Social Issues*, 23: 362–7.

Denham, B. (2000) 'Performance Enhancing Drug Use in Amateur and Professional Sports: Separating the Realities from the Ramblings', *Culture, Sport, Society*, 3: 56–69.

Denham, B. (2004) 'Hero or Hypocrite?: United States and International Media Portrayals of Carl Lewis Amid Revelations of a Positive Drug Test', *International Review for the Sociology of Sport*, 39: 176–85.

Dill, D. B. (1932) 'Studies in muscular activity', *Journal of Physiology*, 77: 49–62.

Dimeo, P. (2006) 'Good Versus Evil? Drugs, Sport and the Cold War', in Wagg, S. and Andrews, D. (eds) *East Plays West: Essays on Sport and the Cold War*, London, Routledge.

Dirix, A. (1966) 'The Doping Problem at the Tokyo and Mexico City Olympic Games', *Journals of Sports Medicine and Physical Fitness*, 6: 183–6.

Dirix, A. (1988) 'Classes and Methods', in Dirix, A., Knuttgen, H. G. and Tittel, K. (eds) *The Olympic Book of Sports Medicine: Volume 1 of the Encyclopaedia of Sports Medicine*, Oxford, Blackwell.

Dirix, A. and Sturbois, X. (1998) *The First Thirty Years of the International Olympic Committee Medical Commission*, Lausanne, IOC.

Docherty, J. K. (1960) 'Modern Amateurism and the Olympic Code', *Bulletin du Comité Internationale Olympique*, February, 69: 63–8.

Donohoe, T. and Johnson, N. (1986) *Foul Play: Drug Abuse in Sports*, Oxford, Basil Blackwell.

Duchaine, D. (1989) *Underground Steroid Users' Handbook II*, Venice, CA, HLR Technical Books.

Dyment, P. G. (1984) 'Drug Use and the Adolescent Athlete', *Pediatric Annals*, 13 (8): 602–4.

Ehrenreich, J. (1978) 'Introduction' in Ehrenreich, J. (ed) *The Cultural Crisis of Modern Medicine*, New York and London, Monthly Review Press.

Fair, J. (1993) 'Isometrics or Steroids? Exploring New Frontiers of Strength in the Early 1960s', *Journal of Sport History*, 20 (1): 1–24.

Fisher, R. G. and Robson, H. E. (1969) '"Doping" in the 1958 Empire and Commonwealth Games', *British Journal of Sports Medicine*, 4 (2): 163–5.

Foltz, E., Ivy, A. C. and Barborka, C. J. (1942) 'The Use of Double Work Periods in the Study of Fatigue and the Influence of Caffeine on Recovery', *American Journal of Physiology*, 136: 79–86.

Fotheringham, W. (2003) *Put Me Back on My Bike: In Search of Tom Simpson*, London, Yellow Jersey Press.

Fowler, W. M., Gardner, G. W. and Egstrom, G. H. (1965) 'Effect of an Anabolic Steroid on Physical Performance of Young Men', *Journal of Applied Physiology*, 20:1038–40.

Freed, D. L. J., and Banks, A. J. (1975) 'A Double-blind Cross-over Trial of Methandienone ("Dianabol") in Moderate Dosage on Highly Trained Experienced Athletes', *British Journal of Sports Medicine*, 9 (2): 78–81.

Fruehan, A. E. and Frawley, T. F. (1963) 'Current Status of Anabolic Steroids', *Journal of the American Medical Association*, 184 (7): 527–32.

Gilbert, B. (1969) 'Drugs in Sport: Problems in a Turned-on World', *Sports Illustrated*, 23 June.

Gold, A. (1986) 'International Policy and Philosophy of Drug Control in Sport', *Drugs Abuse in Sport: Report of a Sports Council Symposium for Governing Bodies, 27 March 1985*, London, Sports Council.

Goldman, B., Klatz, R. and Bush, P. (1984) *Death in the Locker Room*, South Bend, Indiana, Icarus Press.

Goodwin, L. S. (1999) *The Pure Food, Drink and Drugs Crusaders, 1879–1914*, Jefferson, North Carolina, McFarland & Co.

Guardian, 23 August 1972.

Guttmann, A. (1978) *From Ritual to Record: The Nature of Modern Sports*, New York, Columbia University Press.

Guttmann, A. (1984) *The Games Must Go On: Avery Brundage and the Olympic Movement*, New York, Columbia University Press.

Haldi, J. and Wrynn, W. (1946) 'Action of Drugs on Efficiency of Swimmers', *Research Quarterly for the American Physical Education Association*, 17: 96–101.

Haller, J. S. (1973) 'The History of Strychnine in the Nineteenth-Century Materia Medica', *Transactions and Studies of the College of Physicians of Philadelphia*, 40 (4): 226–38.

Haupt, H. A. and Rovere, G. D. (1984) 'Anabolic Steroids: A Review of the Literature', *American Journal of Sports Medicine*, 12 (6): 469–84.

Hellebrandt, F. A. and Karpovich, P. V. (1941) 'Fitness, Fatigue and Recuperation: Survey of Methods Used for Improving the Physical Performance of Man', *War Medicine*, 1 (6): 745–68.

Hervey, G. R. (1975) 'Are athletes wrong about anabolic steroids?', *British Journal of Sports Medicine*, 9 (2): 74–7.

Herxheimer, H. (1922) 'Zur Wirkung des Koffeins auf die sportliche Leistung', *Moenchen Med Wochenschr*, 69: 1339.

Hoberman, J. (1986) *The Olympic Crisis: Sport, Politics and the Moral Order*, New York, Caratzas.

Hoberman, J. (1992) *Mortal Engines: The Science of Performance and the Dehumanization of Sport*, New York, Free Press.

Hoberman, J. (2003) '"A Pharmacy on Wheels": Doping and Community Cohesion among Professional Cyclists Following the Tour de France', in Møller, V. and Nauright, J. (eds) *The Essence of Sport*, Odense, University of Southern Denmark Press.

Hoberman, J. (2005) *Testosterone Dreams: Rejuvenation, Aphrodisia, Doping*, Berkeley, California, University of California Press.

Hoffman, B. (1967) 'Anabolics', *Strength and Health*, 35, October.

Hollyhock, M. (1969) 'The Application of Drugs to Modify Human Performance', *British Journal of Sports Medicine*, 4 (2): 119–27.

Holt, R. (1992) *Sport and the British: A Modern History*, Oxford, Clarendon Press.

Houlihan, B. (1999) *Dying to Win: Doping in Sport and the Development of Anti-doping Policy*, Strasbourg, Council of Europe.

Howard, V. (1991) 'Fair Play: Ethical Issues of Doping in Sport', in Laura, R. S. and White, S. W. (eds) *Drug Controversy in Sport: The Socio-Ethical and Medical Issues*, Sydney, Allen & Unwin.

IOC (1938) *Bulletin Officiel du Comité International Olympique*, July 1938, no. 37.

IOC (1964) 63rd IOC Session Minutes, 6–10 October 1964.

IOC (1967) 65th IOC Session Minutes, May 6–9 1967.

IOC (1968) 67th IOC Session Minutes, 7–11 October 1968.

IOC (1969a) Executive Board Minutes, 26–31 January 1969.

IOC (1969b) Executive Board Minutes, 22–23 March 1969.

IOC (1970a) Executive Board Minutes, 3–4 October 1970.

IOC (1970b) Executive Board Minutes, 13–14 March 1970.

IOC (1971) 71st IOC Session Minutes, 15–17 September 1971.

IOC (1973) Executive Board Minutes, 2–5 February 1973.

IOC (1999) *Doping: An International White Paper*, Lausanne, IOC.

Ivy, A. C. and Krasno, L. R. (1941) 'Amphetamine (Benzedrine) Sulphate: A Review of its Pharmacology', *War Medicine*, 1 (1): 15–42.

Johnson, L. C. and O'Shea, J. P. (1969) 'Anabolic Steroids: Effect on Strength Development', *Science*, 164 (2): 957–9.

Jones, P. V. C. (1908) 'Effect of Strychnine on Muscular Work', *Journal of Physiology*, 36: 435–46.

Joy, B. (1952) *Forward Arsenal! A History of Arsenal Football Club*, London, Phoenix House.

Karpovich, P. (1941) 'Ergogenic Aids in Work and Sport', *Research Quarterly for the American Physical Education Association*, 12 (2): 432–50.

Kato, K. (ed) (1964) *Proceedings of International Congress of Sport Sciences 1964*, Tokyo, The Japanese Union of Sport Sciences.

Kicman, A. and Gower, D. B. (2003) 'Anabolic Steroids in Sport: Biochemical, Clinical and Analytical Perspectives', *Annals of Clinical Biochemistry*, 40 (4): 321–56.

Killanin, M. (1983) *My Olympic Years*, London, Secker & Warburg.

Knighton, L. (1948) *Behind the Scenes in Big Football*, London, Stanley Paul & Co.

Knoefel, P. K. (1943) 'The Influence of Phenisopropyl Amine and Phenisoprophyl Methyl Amine on Work Output', *Federation Proceedings*, 2: 83.

Kohn, M. (1992) *Dope Girls: The Birth of the British Drug Underground*, London, Lawrence & Wishart.

La Cava, G. (1962) 'The Use of Drugs in Competitive Sport', *Bulletin du Comité International Olympique*, May, 78: 52–3.

Landry, F, and Yerlès, M. (1996) *The International Olympic Committee: One Hundred Years. The Idea, the Presidents, the Achievements*, 3, Lausanne, IOC.

Laura, R. S. and White, S. W. (1991) 'The Price Athletes Pay in Pursuit of Olympic Gold', in Laura, R. S. and White, S. W. (eds) *Drug Controversy in Sport: The Socio-Ethical and Medical Issues*, Sydney, Allen & Unwin.

Lehman, G. *et al.* (1939) 'Pervitan als Leistungsssteigerndes mittel', *Arbeitsphysiologie*, 10: 680–91.

Lenehan, P. (2003) *Anabolic Steroids*, London and New York, Taylor & Francis.

Lucas, C. (1905) *The Olympic Games 1904*, St. Louis, Mo., Woodward & Tiernan.

Lukas, S. (1985) *Amphetamines: Danger in the Fast Lane*, London, Burke.

Mandell, A. (1976) *The Nightmare Season*, New York, Random House.

Mantegazza, P. (1859/1975) 'Coca Experiences', reproduced in Andrews, G. and Solomon, D. (eds) *The Coca Leaf and Cocaine Papers*, New York and London, Harcourt Brace Jovanovich.

Mayes, H. (1967) *World Cup Report 1966: Written and Compiled for the Football Association*, London, William Heinemann.

McArdle, W. D., Katch, F. I. and Katch, V. L. (2000) *Essentials of Exercise Physiology*, 2nd edn, Baltimore, Lippincott, Williams and Wilkins.

McDonald Bailey, E. (1953) *If It's Speed You're After*, London, Stanley Paul.

McGee, L. C. (1927) 'The Effect of Injection of a Lipoid Fraction of Bull Testicle in Capons', *Proceedings of the Institute of Medicine*, vol. 6.

McNab, T. (1993) 'Why Do Competitors Take Drugs?', *The 4th Permanent World Conference on Anti-Doping in Sport, 5–8 September 1993, Conference Proceedings*, London, Sports Council.

Miah, A. (2004) *Genetically Modified Athletes: Biomedical Ethics, Gene Doping and Sport*, London and New York, Routledge.

Møller, V. (2003) 'What is Sport: Outline to a Redefinition', in Møller, V. and Nauright, J. (eds) *The Essence of Sport*, Odense, University of Southern Denmark Press.

Møller, V. (2005) 'Knud Enemark Jensen's Death During the 1960 Rome Olympics: A Search for Truth?', *Sport in History*, 25 (3): 452–71.

Monaghan, L. (2001) *Bodybuilding, Drugs and Risk*, London and New York, Routledge.

Morning Post, 29 November 1897.

Mullegg, G. and Montandon, H. (1951) 'The Danish Oarsmen who Took Part in the European Championships at Milan in 1950: Were they Drugged?, *Bulletin du Comité International Olympique*, July, 28: 25–6.

Müller, N. (ed.) (2000) *Pierre de Coubertin, 1863–1937. Olympism: selected writings*, Lausanne: IOC.

New York Times, 1 December 1895.

New York Times, 16 December 1900.

New York Times, 25 July 1908.

New York Times, 4 October 1908.

New York Times, 30 March 1926.

New York Times, 17 February, 1927.

New York Times, 24 December, 1942.

New York Times, 1 October, 1948.

New York Times, 26 February 1952.

New York Times, 2 August 1952.

New York Times, 7 June 1957.

New York Times, 8 June 1957.

New York Times, 28 May 1959.

New York Times, 24 January 1971.

New York Times, 17 October 1971.

New York Times, 14 July 1973.

News of the World, 26 February 1939.

News of the World, 7 May 1939.

Nicholson, G. (1978) *The Great Bike Race*, London, Magnum.

Novich, M. (1964) 'Use and Misuse of Drugs to Improve Athletic Performance', in Kato, K. (ed.) *Proceedings of International Congress of Sport Sciences 1964*, Tokyo, The Japanese Union of Sport Sciences.

O'Malley, P. and Valverde, M. (2004) 'Pleasure, Freedom and Drugs: The Uses of "Pleasure" in Liberal Governance of Drug and Alcohol Consumption, *Sociology*, 38 (1): 25–42.

O'Shea, J. (1970) 'Anabolic Steroids: Effect on Competitive Swimmers', *Nutrition Reports International*, 1: 337–42.

O'Shea, J. (1971) 'The Effects of an Anabolic Steroid on Dynamic Strength Levels of Weightlifters', *Nutrition Reports International*, 4: 363–70.

O'Shea, J. and Winkler, W. (1970) 'Biochemical and Physical Effects of an Anabolic Steroid in Competitive Swimmers and Weightlifters', *Nutrition Report International*, 2: 351–62.

Oslin, R. (2006) 'Connolly a Statuesque Figure in BC Lore', *Boston College Chronicle*, 2 February.

Outing (1896) 'A New Factor in Athletics: the banishment of fatigue', XXVIII, 3: 214–20.

Oza, G. M. (1969) 'Athletes, Doping and Olympism', *Olympic Review*, April, 19: 209–12.

Oza, G. M. (1971) 'The Olympic Ideal Faces Extinction, *Olympic Review*, March, 42: 179–80.

Payne, A. H. (1975) 'Anabolic steroids in athletics ("The Rise of the Mediocrity")', *British Journal of Sports Medicine*, 9 (2): 83–8.

Pierson, W. R. (1971) 'Amphetamine Sulphate and Performance: a critique', *Journal of the American Medical Association*, 177(5): 345–7.

Pikhala, L. (1930) 'Allgemeine Richtlinien für das athletische Training', in Krümel, C. (ed.) *Athletik: Ein Handbuch der lebenswichtigen Leibesübengen*, Munich, pp. 185–90.

Pirie, G. (1961) *Running Wild*, London, W. H. Allen.

Poppelreuter, W. (1930) 'Ist die Einnahme von primärem Natriumphosphat ein Dopingmittel?', *Die Leibesübungen*, p. 534.

Porritt, A. (1965) 'Doping', *Journal of Sports Medicine and Physical Fitness*, 5 (3): 166–8.

Porritt, A. (1969) ' Doping in Sport', *British Journal of Sports Medicine*, 4 (2): 105–8.

Pottage, J. C. (1891) *Kola: Its History and Characteristics*, Edinburgh, Lorimer & Gillies.

Pound, R. W. (2004) *Inside the Olympics: A Behind-the-scenes Look at the Politics, the Scandals, and the Glory of the Games*, Toronto, Wiley.

Prokop, L. (1966) 'The Problem of Doping', in Kato, K. (ed.) *Proceedings of International Congress of Sport Sciences, 1964*, Tokyo, The Japanese Union of Sport Sciences.

Prokop, L. (1975) 'Drug Abuse in International Athletics', *Journal of Sport Medicine*, 3 (2): 85–7.

Rabinbach, A. (1992) *The Human Motor: Energy, Fatigue, and the Origins of Modernity*, Berkeley and Los Angeles, California, University of California Press.

Raynes, R. H. (1969) 'The Doping of Athletes', *British Journal of Sports Medicine*, 4 (2): 145–62.

Reisser, O. (1930) 'Ist medikamentöse Beeinflussung im Sport möglich?', *Die Leibesübungen*, p. 537.

Reisser, O. (1933) 'Über Doping und Dopingmittel', *Leibesübungen und körperliche Erziehung*, pp. 393–4.

Reiterer, W. (2000) *Positive: An Australian Olympian Reveals the Inside Story of Drugs and Sport*, Sydney, Pan McMillan.

Riordan, J. (1991) *Sport, Politics and Communism*, Manchester, Manchester University Press.

Riordan, J. (1993) 'The Rise and Fall of Soviet Olympic Champions', *Olympika: The International Journal of Olympic Studies*, 2: 25–44.

Ritchie, I. (2003) 'Sex Tested, Gender Verified: Controlling Female Sexuality in the Age of Containment', *Sport History Review*, 34 (1): 80–98.

Rivers, W. H. R. (1908) *The Influence of Alcohol and Other Drugs on Fatigue: The Croonian Lectures Delivered at the Royal College of Physicians in 1906*, London, Edward Arnold.

Rudolf, G. (1947) 'The Effect of Amphetamine on Fatigue and Depression', *British Journal of Addiction*, 44 (2): 71–3.

Santos, J. and Pini, M. 'Doping' (1963), *Bulletin du Comité International Olympique*, February, 1963, 81: 56–7.

Saunders, F. S. (1999) *Who Paid the Piper? The CIA and the Cultural Cold War*, London, Granta.

Schantz, O. (1995) 'The Presidency of Avery Brundage, 1952–1972', in *The International Olympic Committee – One Hundred Years, Part II*, Lausanne, IOC.

Scott, J. (1971) 'It's Not How You Play the Game, But What Pill You Take', *New York Times*, 17 October.

Simonsen, E., Kearns, W.C. and Enzer, N. (1944) 'Effect of Methyl Testosterone Treatment on Muscular Performance and the Central Nervous System of Older Men', *Journal of Clinical Endocrinology*, 4: 528–34.

Sports Council (1986) *Drugs Abuse in Sport: Report of the Sports Council Symposium for Governing Bodies*, London, Sports Council.

Sumner, N.A. (1974) 'Measurement of Anabolic Steroids by Radioimmunoassay', *Journal of Steroid Biochemistry*, 5 (4): 307.

Sunday People, 13 September 1964.

Sunday Telegraph, 13 September 1964.

Taylor, D. J. (2006) *On the Corinthian Spirit: The Decline of Amateurism in Sport*, London, Yellow Jersey Press.

Taylor, F. W. (1911) *The Principles of Scientific Management*, New York, Harper.

Taylor, W. (1985) *Hormonal Manipulation: A New Era of Monstrous Athletes*, London, McFarland.

Taylor, W. (1991) *Macho Medicine: A History of the Anabolic Steroid Epidemic*, London, McFarland and Co.

Theil, D. and Essing, B. (1930) 'Cocain und Muskelarbeit. I. Der Einfluss auf Leistung und Gasstoffwechsel', *Arbeitsphysiologie*, 3: 287–97.

The Times, 24 July 1896.

The Times, 15 May 1897.

The Times, 10 December 1897.

The Times, 6 June 1957

The Times, 12 September 1964.

The Times, 10 September 1968.

The Times, 15 April 1970.

The Times, 17 July 1970.

The Times, 21 April 1972.

The Times, 24 August 1972.

The Times, 14 October, 1972.

The Times, 27 November 1972.

The Times, 1 November 1973.

Todd, T. (1987) 'Anabolic Steroids: The Gremlins of Sport', *Journal of Sport History*, 14 (1): 87–107.

Todd, T. (1992) ' A History of the Use of Anabolic Steroids in Sport' in Berryman, J. and Park, R. (eds) *Sport and Exercise Science: Essays in the History of Sports Medicine*, Urbana, University of Illinois Press.

Toohey, K. and Veal, A. J. (2000) *The Olympic Games: A Social Science Perspective*, Wallingford and New York, CABI.

Trory, E. (1980) *Munich, Montreal and Moscow: A Political Tale of Three Olympic Cities*, Hove, Crabtree.

Ungerleider, S. (2001) *Faust's Gold: Inside the East German Doping Machine*, New York, St. Martin's Press.

Venerando, A. (1964) 'Italian Experiments on the Pathology of Doping and Ways to Control It', *Appendix to Council of Europe Committee for Out-of-School Education, Doping of Athletes: Reports of the Special Working Parties*, Strasbourg, Council of Europe, pp. 47–53.

Voet, W. (2001) *Breaking the Chain: Drugs and Cycling – the True Story*, London, Yellow Jersey Press.

Voy, R. (1988) 'Clinical Aspects of the Doping Classes', in Dirix, A., Knuttgen, H. G. and Tittel, K. (eds) *The Olympic Book of Sports Medicine*, Oxford, Blackwell.

Voy, R. (1991) *Drugs, Sport and Politics*, Champaign, Il., Leisure Press.

Waddington, I. (2000) *Sport, Health and Drugs: A Critical Sociological Perspective*, London, Spon.

Waddington, I. (2005) 'Changing Patterns of Drug Use in British Sport from the 1960s', *Sport in History*, 25 (3): 472–96.

Ward, R. J., Shackleton, C. H., and Lawson, A. M. (1975) 'Gas Chromatographic-mass Spectrometric Methods for the Detection and Identification of Anabolic Steroid Drugs', *British Journal of Sports Medicine*, 9: 93–7.

Wheatcroft, G. (2003) *Le Tour: A History of the Tour de France*, London, Simon & Schuster.

Whittaker, T. (1938) 'Will Science Give Us ROBOT ATHLETES?', *News of the World*, 2 April.

Williams, J. G. P. (1963) 'Doping of Athletes', *Physical Education*, 55 (165): 39–41.

Williams, J. G. P. (1969) 'Dope in British Sport', *British Journal of Sports Medicine*, 4 (2): 128–33.

Williams, M. H. (1974) *Drugs and Athletic Performance*, Springfield, Il., Charles C. Thomas.

Woodland, L. (1980) *Dope: The Use of Drugs in Sport*, Newton Abbot and London, David and Charles.

Woodland, L. (2003) *The Crooked Path to Victory: Drugs and Cheating in Professional Bicycling Racing*, San Francisco, Cycle Publishing.

Wright, J. (1978) *Anabolic Steroids and Sports*, Natick, MA, Sports Science Consultant.

Yarborough, C. (1899) 'Therapeutics of Kola', *Journal of the American Medical Association*, 33: 1148–9, reprinted in *Journal of the American Medical Association*, 282 (20): 1898.

Yesalis, C., Kennedy, N., Kopstein, A. and Bahrke, M. (1993) 'Anabolic-androgenic Steroid Use in the United States', *Journal of the American Medical Association*, 270, (10): 1217–21.

Zeigler, J. (1984) 'Introduction', in Goldman, B., Klatz, R. and Bush, P., *Death in the Locker Room*, South Bend, Indiana, Icarus Press.

Index